Praise for *The Inc*
and **Mason Donovan and Mark Kaplan**

"Diversity, like corporate social responsibility, is one of those buzz concepts that managers love to promote, despite not knowing how it fits into a company's strategic vision . . . It's rare to find a business book that so soundly hits the zeitgeist while also capably applying the best social sciences research to an important topic."

—*Publishers Weekly*

"An insightful read. *The Inclusion Dividend* sheds light on core concepts for understanding diversity and inclusion dynamics and provides strategies for organizations to realize inclusion's full impact on the bottom line."

—Edith Hunt, Chief Diversity Officer, Goldman Sachs

"Diversity is a priority for the twenty-first century. *The Inclusion Dividend*, in its revised edition, is an essential tool to help people managers and diversity leaders understand, through an evidence-based approach, create innovative diversity, equity and inclusion strategies for future workforce. A playbook for the entire organization."

—Ana Duarte McCarthy, Director, Forte Foundation

"Kaplan and Donovan help remove the veil of mystery that shrouds inclusion. *The Inclusion Dividend* provides a much-needed narrative for organizations to rethink and reposition their journey toward ingraining sustainable diversity and closing the intent-impact inclusion chasm—the end goal being the holy grail of pure meritocracy for all."

—Nia Joynson-Romanzina, Former Global Head of Diversity & Inclusion, Swiss Reinsurance Company

"*The Inclusion Dividend* is the diversity and inclusion conversation of tomorrow we should be having with our business leaders today. This is a book to be shared with the entire organization."

—Kate Vernon, Director of Strategy & Communications, Community Business

"*The Inclusion Dividend* is a journey that takes us beyond the fatigued word *diversity*. Looking at the importance of inclusiveness, higher levels of engagement, and understanding our biases is crucial to talent management overall. Kaplan and Donovan continue to provide a refreshing view on lessons learned from some of the best in the global business world."

—Nancy J. Di Dia, CEO and president of Di Dia Diversity Consulting Group, LLC and Chief Diversity Officer, Fortune 500 company

"As future historians look to identify the impetus for global cultural change in the early 21st century, they will count this book among the factors for that change. *The Inclusion Dividend* provides takeaways and key points that are factual, informative, and stimulating. The stories and examples challenge us to translate diversity and inclusion into action. . . . a critical read for anyone seeking to affect positive change in a diverse and inclusive global society."

—Carolyn Jones, Director of Diversity and Inclusion, Raytheon Global Business

THE
INCLUSION
DIVIDEND

THE
INCLUSION
DIVIDEND

Why Investing in
DIVERSITY & INCLUSION
Pays Off

MASON DONOVAN

MARK KAPLAN

Published by DG Press

PO Box 172

Salisbury, NH 03268

Tel: 603-796-2028

www.TheDagobaGroup.com

Printed in the United States of America

ISBN   978-1-7327262-0-8 (paperback)

ISBN   978-1-7327262-1-5 (ebook)

Contents

Preface to the Second Edition

A lot has happened on the sociopolitical front since we completed the first edition of ***The Inclusion Dividend*** in 2013. The second term of the first African American president ended with the first woman to lead a major party presidential ticket losing to the oldest candidate to start his first term as president. The presidential campaign was marked by divisiveness and strong disagreements about diversity in the country. "Identity politics" has emerged in a more all-encompassing way, and fear and polarization are on full display. This dynamic is not limited to the United States; we see it in many parts of the world. In the wake of this growing sociopolitical dynamic, colleagues and clients have asked if we think the field of diversity and inclusion (D&I) will suffer in the wake of a public discourse that seems at times hostile toward diversity and inclusion. When we were asked in 2016, we thought not, and we continue to feel that way. Our firm, The Dagoba Group, has fielded more requests for work since 2016 than ever before.

In fact, in our view, the current environment has brought a mini-surge in diversity-focused awareness education. We saw this early in 2016, with both the corporate pressure to change state-level anti-LGBT laws and the greater visibility of incidents of police violence toward African Americans and the social activism that resulted. More and more organizations are having direct conversations about race, in ways that are similar to past awareness training but also urgent in a different way.

We've seen the power of a much-denied public voice embodied in the #MeToo movement, and how that has forced organizations to take a sober look at their culture.

We believe this mini-surge may represent an inflection point in the multi-decade effort to create more inclusive organizations and institutions. Often, what seems like a step backward translates to two steps forward. Social change frequently proceeds this way. The great leap forward of LGBT inclusion, for example, occurred faster than many expected, and at a time when social conservatism seemed to be making a comeback, or at least holding its own. And then, to some, it seemed that marriage equality became the law of the land overnight.

So why are we making progress on diversity and inclusion at a time when the nation seems so divisive and polarized?

We believe there are three primary reasons: inevitability, progress, and necessity. Diversity, at least, is inevitable. As a nation, we've been heading down this road almost since our inception, and the trend has accelerated in the last few decades. We simply are going to be diverse, increasingly so, and the only question is how inclusive we will be and how quickly. But even inclusion is inevitable, short of a complete revolution of our legal system. Progress has been sure, though slow at times. Measures of public attitudes over the past fifty years reflect a growing awareness, tolerance, and acceptance of greater diversity. We have become more aware but also more effective, and this shows in the growth of an increasingly diverse group of leaders across almost all institutions and organizations, public, private, and nonprofit. Necessity is the driver we haven't fully acknowledged at a societal level, but institutions are seeing it. In an increasingly global and multicultural context, we simply must become more inclusive if we are going to treat patients, serve customers, build effective strategies, and more fully utilize our human resources.

What should you do?

We believe the next phase in D&I work is already upon us. We see it in the requests that come from clients. They are asking us less about proving the value of D&I, as that is already well established. Instead, they want to know how to embed inclusiveness into what they do. They are integrating inclusiveness and applying it on multiple fronts, to processes, strategies, and decisions that aren't overtly about D&I. They are building inclusiveness into their day-to-day interactions and team environments.

The Inclusion Dividend has been more successful than we ever anticipated. It is now a core textbook in colleges and universities throughout North America, listed as a corporate must-read for leaders, and featured at symposiums around the world. None of this would have transpired if inclusion was not connected to success in most, if not all, important endeavors, from those of our society, to our government's, to those of public and private organizations. Long-developing demographic shifts have combined with the interconnectedness of most everything we do to highlight the critical contributions of people all across the human spectrum. We have passed the point of no return, and a huge opportunity is revealing itself. In this second edition, we have updated the statistics and studies, clarified points, and provided additional concepts. D&I is a journey with many roads. Read on, and see how you can be on the front edge of this inevitable change.

Acknowledgments

Our approach to the work of diversity and inclusion has been shaped by many mentors and colleagues, a number of whom were pioneers in this field. At the top of that list is Elsie Cross, a woman whose approach invited us to look deep inside ourselves to understand the complex and emotional issues of discrimination, oppression, and change. She invited many onto a life-changing path. Elsie and her peers were a generation of change agents who literally created a field of work in corporate America. Work in Elsie's organization connected dozens of highly skilled professionals, and we are grateful for their leadership. While not able to name everyone, we must acknowledge Delyte Frost, Shirley Fletcher, Denise Matteucci, Curt Waller, Toni Dunton-Butler, and Barbara Riley as exceptional leaders and teachers. Everything that we have written in this book is a blend of their influence, client interactions, and our own life experiences.

We thank Bill Paige for helping us understand via Thomas Jefferson, the need to hold paradoxical notions. We have been pushed, shaped, prodded, and loved by many colleagues throughout our learning journey.

Our families created an environment of unconditional love where we were given the freedom to be ourselves, and we were taught, often implicitly, to support the underdog. Somewhere Mark still has the photo of his Aunt Linda Kaplan Kielek at a human rights rally in the '70s.

Incidentally, Mason's father still has his first human rights card from a time when fighting for basic equality was not as accepted as it is today. While we didn't quite replicate their social activism, we were inspired to challenge assumptions and become instruments of change.

Lastly, none of this could have come together without our partnership. Just after we wrote the original edition of this book, marriage equality became law throughout the United States. We married in late 2013, and we believe this basic human right adds value to our nation and contributes to the inclusion dividend our country continues to realize.

Introduction

Asha received her mutual fund prospectus in the mail. For the last five years, she has diligently dedicated a small percentage of her salary to a select grouping of funds. When she first started, she studied all of the types of funds within her company's plan. There were the "safe" funds, which invested in government bonds with a low but reliable rate of return. On the other end of the spectrum were aggressive growth funds investing in global start-ups, which involved a much higher degree of risk. One of these funds had some amazing returns when it did well and steep negative returns during the really bad years.

Asha was advised to diversify her money wisely over a portfolio of funds that matched her particular financial goals. She was told by her financial professional that diversity was the key to a healthy portfolio. Every month she received a report on how well the funds performed. And every month she wanted to readjust the distribution of her money based on the funds' recent success or failure. It was not too long before she realized that obsessing about the short-term ups and downs was not a good strategy. She needed to take a longer view. With the right approach, patience, and proper metrics, she would realize the dividends on her investment.

Asha was a divisional director of research and development at a large pharmaceutical company. Her department had recently grown because her company had decided to shift its product line more toward animal medication, her department's area of specialty. She had an appointment with the department's new recruiting manager and was waiting outside the office while an interview was finishing up. She picked up a magazine on diversity in the workplace and started to read an article about how Frito-Lay leveraged diversity to grow a segment of its snack business by $100 million. Frito-Lay's employee resource groups were active with product R&D ideas, and in fact Adelante, the Latino employee resource group, had been instrumental in creating the guacamole chip. In the same publication, she saw a reference to multiple studies that show a strong correlation between the presence of a more diverse demographic in management roles and strong company performance.

Asha then read other anecdotes about how investment in creating a diverse and inclusive workplace provided a dividend to the business. She scratched her head and thought about how she had historically perceived her company's diversity efforts as a corporate compliance challenge. Asha just wanted good people, and honestly felt it did not matter what else you brought to the table as long as you were good at your job. Admittedly, her team was almost all white and male. They were good employees who did their jobs well. Yes, they were falling behind one of their competitors and were being nipped at the heels by recent upstarts. She "knew" that had nothing to do with the lack of diversity on her team or how "inclusive" the culture felt. Yet, reading these stories about how inclusion efforts have provided dividends made Asha think back to her initial 401k days.

A dividend is something that you get when you make an investment. It pays out over time, and sometimes it is very small in the beginning. If reinvested, it compounds and eventually provides exponential growth. An essentially conservative strategy, it is the most time-honored and valued long-term investment approach.

When she first began investing, she really didn't see how a few dollars every week would ever amount to much. All of the paperwork, choices, and up-front financial drain felt a little overwhelming. Asha did her research and decided that weekly investment was the best path to take. Five years later, with the right investment strategy, she looks back at that decision as the foundation of a comfortable retirement. She understands that any return requires investment, but she is still leery about how investing in diversity and inclusion beyond legal compliance could help her company or, more pointedly, herself.

If you share some similarities with Asha, then you made the right choice to pick up this book. *The Inclusion Dividend* was written for business leaders trying to better understand how their personal and corporate investment in inclusion will provide a return. You are not expected to have a command of the terminology or methodology; you will gain that in this book.

Over three decades of working with corporations around the world, we have found that a strategic investment in creating a diverse and inclusive corporate culture always pays off. It pays off at the individual level with happier, more fulfilled employees, at the group/team level with increased productivity and innovation, and at the systemic level with additional bottom-line shareholder value. Shortly after Mark earned his MA in HR development, he began his career working in the diversity and inclusion field almost thirty years ago; first as an employee for a corporation and then as an independent consultant. Mason followed a different path and earned his MA in international business before jumping into sales management and marketing. While Mark established an expertise in fostering inclusive workplaces, Mason focused on developing award-winning sales teams. It is this dynamic combination which allows us to couple the best in class D&I approach with a corporate ROI lens.

Just as Asha approached her 401k investment strategy by doing some research, we will start this book's first chapter with some background information to give you a better handle on the evolution of diversity and inclusion in the workplace. We will also discuss key terms, to give you a foundation in the vocabulary. Next, we'll touch upon the various dimensions of difference most popularly connected to diversity and inclusion (D&I). Finally, we'll address some of the challenges to creating a truly inclusive culture.

Chapter 2 dives right into the business case. As a good businessperson, you are looking for the multiplier effect. In other words, you want to know how your $1 investment will return $5, $10, or $20 in increased revenues or decreased costs. We will explore the business case internally (innovation, retention, morale, productivity, etc.) and externally (client engagement, increased revenue, market growth, etc.). Every company is unique, so you will need to bring your ideas to the table to see where you, your group, or the entire company may have the best business case.

After presenting the business case for an inclusive culture, the next step is to dive into the key concepts for inclusion and how these concepts are felt at different levels in the organizations. Chapters 3 and 4 introduce core ideas about inclusion efforts, and take concepts that can be complicated and apply them directly to your daily work life, allowing you to fully grasp how they come in to play. The stories we provide in the chapters throughout this book are based on true cases, but we have altered names and a few details to maintain anonymity. Given the way these stories repeat themselves from industry to industry, company to company, and group to group, you will no doubt think we are speaking about your company. Even in a world of difference, we have so much in common.

In chapters 5, 6, and 7, we take you deeper into three areas of workplace dynamics: unconscious bias, insider–outsider dynamics, and dimensions of difference. In our experience, leaders who have a greater awareness of these three areas can champion a more sustainable culture of inclusion. As in other chapters, we provide real stories to bring these concepts to life.

Having all of this knowledge is great. However, knowing how to make a better lightbulb and having an executable plan to do it are two different things. The last two chapters speak to leadership competencies, tools for inclusion, and long-term strategy. As with Asha's mutual funds, some will provide short-term returns while others will help you reach your long-term destination. Knowing where to place your investment, how to measure the return, and when to change direction are critical to a successful approach.

At the end of each chapter we provide you with some takeaways and invite you to apply them to the case study and/or questions provided. The book can be used as the basis for a group discussion or read individually. It does not require you to read sequentially. Feel free to jump from one chapter to the next, depending on your interests or current situation.

This book is not intended to substitute for in-person development. It should be used as a primer or as a supplement. Inclusion is a journey to be taken, in person, with others. This book is simply a road map to help you on your way.

Lastly, we ask you to keep a journal. We would love to hear about your stories. Email us at **Info@TheDagobaGroup.com**.

1

Diversity? Inclusion? What Do We Mean?

About twenty-five years ago, Mark's father asked him, "So what do you do anyhow?" This question started an interesting internal dialogue. How do you talk about this work? The topic is a result of a difficult, contentious, and emotionally loaded history. In the United States it goes back to the founding documents and the notion that every citizen has a right to "life, liberty, and the pursuit of happiness." It is also in the last line of the Pledge of Allegiance: "with liberty and justice for all." Yet diversity and inclusion work also falls under the corporate-speak of "organizational change," "consulting," and "leadership development." "Diversity" can mean so many different things, including the innumerable ways in which human beings are different. "Inclusion" is a generic term, implying everything from how welcome we feel to leveraging diversity to sentiments like "Can't we all just get along?" We hope to narrow the focus a bit for you.

Three words you will read and hear a lot in our discussion need defining. Meritocracy, inclusion, and diversity all go hand in glove. It is not uncommon for inclusion and diversity to be used interchangeably or as one entity. This usage is incorrect. Although they are very closely connected, they require distinct definitions.

We will begin the conversation with a notion most executives believe is firmly embedded in the corporate culture: meritocracy. Later in the chapter, we'll review a very brief history of the origins of diversity and inclusion (D&I) in the corporate sector and describe some common challenges in creating an inclusive environment.

Our perspective is somewhat US-centric when it comes to the history of diversity and inclusion. The United States has a unique history and is, in many ways, the leader in advancing the D&I conversation in organizations. Although there are distinct differences globally, as we provide development around the world we have found quite a few commonalities. The concepts and processes we talk about in this book are applicable globally, and we will speak with a global voice from time to time.

As employees of the twenty-first century, all of us live in three worlds of D&I that can seem to be incompatible at times. There is the civil world, which revolves around legislation regarding issues like marriage rights, equality of access, and equitable treatment. Then there is the academic world, where a theoretical debate persists across the fields of law, sociology, psychology, and equality and fairness in employment. Should the law favor some groups over others? Is everyone biased and, if so, how should we account for that? What is a fair way to create a level playing field? What is a fair expectation of private employers? Finally, there is the corporate world. As students become employees, it is the corporate world that absorbs eight or more hours of their waking time most days, and the discussion is more narrowly focused on the best ways to create personal and corporate growth.

Although the corporate world is greatly influenced by civil reality, corporations can, at times, be ahead of legislation. For example, many corporations had offered same-sex domestic partner benefits long before regional civil laws required it. The reason for this forward thinking is often based on a clear link between D&I and the effectiveness and/or profitability of the organization, often called "the business case"—a topic we have devoted an entire chapter to detailing. There are times when movements in the wider culture can greatly influence the corporate space. Between the initial publication of this book and this edition, several rights movements have altered the corporate conversation. Black Lives Matter, #MeToo, and the fight for transgender rights are among the movements that have been addressed at a corporate level and that we will weave throughout our discussion in this book. The entirety of this book is focused on the corporate world, although the lessons are applicable in other realms.

After the history lesson, we provide some common challenges to building an inclusive workplace: structural challenges, process challenges, and human challenges. Structural challenges are about the roots of the company, the type of industry, and what is "baked into the cake" from the creation of the organization. Process challenges are about the main people challenges of running any company: talent acquisition, talent management, and leadership. The human challenges include leadership, but also the human dynamics of working effectively across difference. These include unconscious bias and group dynamics.

While the internal challenges are structural, process, and human, they also have an impact at the interface between the organization and its stakeholders; the marketplace, which consists of customers and communities, is likely the chief stakeholder for most organizations. We briefly touch on these challenges and go into more detail in future chapters. Lastly, we will explore the dimensions of difference that are the corporate focus today and look toward where we will be tomorrow.

A Word About Intent

Our thirty years of experience with leaders of large global companies have taught us that most leaders intend to be inclusive. What leader wouldn't want to have a more inclusive organization, where meritocracy is alive and well and where the best potential and performance are being tapped? At an individual level, many of these leaders believe in equality and fairness. For the most part, they wouldn't want to restrict the opportunities of others.

Arguing, implicitly or explicitly, that leaders are consciously biased evokes defensiveness and slows change in creating inclusive organizations. Helping leaders to see that bias is often unconscious and unintentional is a more productive starting point. Not only is this contention supported by substantial recent research on perceptions, bias, and how the brain functions, it also offers a more empowering way of moving forward. It does not remove the critical role that leaders must play in creating change, nor does it remove their responsibility in challenging the status quo. It removes some blame and defensiveness from the equation, however, and that helps the process of change. The challenge presented in this book is less about intent and more about the actual impact of behavior, policies, practices, and organizational culture. The dividend is in the resulting impact. The real challenge, for society and for organizations, is matching the good intent with the actual impact at every level.

To get the most out of this book, you will need to embrace the concept of multiple realities, some of which seem contradictory and paradoxical. For example, we are firm believers (just as we think most companies are) in the notion of individuality, and we believe that all people need to be treated as individuals. We also believe that sometimes our group identities as female or male, baby boomer or millennial, white or people of color, and so on have significant impact on our experiences in organizations, sometimes even more than our individual identities. We embrace both individuality and "groupness," and suggest that you should too.

We think you should also consider that a leader's intent does not always match the impact that his actions have. It may seem paradoxical to accept the notion that your company is doing some fantastic things—being wildly successful, meritocratic, and inclusive—while at the same time perpetuating discrimination and unequal treatment, and failing to tap important resources across the organization. Our colleague Bill Paige, a great admirer of Thomas Jefferson, describes Jefferson as a great paradox, a man who was writing one of the most powerful documents on individual liberty and freedom at the same time he owned several hundred human beings as slaves. The goal is to bring actual impact in line with good intent. This end is not always easy to achieve, but it can be reached with a dedicated, smart, and strategic approach. Full and systemic inclusion is a worthy goal, but it is one that most organizations are unlikely to realize without concerted effort.

The leadership challenge is to understand the gap between where you are and where you want to be and use that "creative tension," as Peter Senge calls it, as the catalyst for change. We offer one more paradox for you to embrace as a leader. We will talk about this in more detail later, but if you are a leader you are likely a member of many "insider" groups—certainly by your level in the organization but possibly also by your age, ability, class, culture, gender, race, sexual orientation, and so on. The dynamics of inclusion predict that while you may have the most power to create change in the organization you likely know the least about what needs to be changed—at least on the surface. This is because you've never had to think about it unless you chose to. By reading this book, perhaps you are choosing consciously to better understand inclusion.

A Long-Cherished Notion

A person starts a small business in the garage, kitchen, or apartment. Through long hours, hard work, and a little bit of luck they build this business into a multibillion-dollar enterprise. Sound familiar? This could be the story of Jim Casey, who started the American Messenger

Company with a couple of bikes and help from his brothers. Over the years, this company transformed into one of the best-known global icons, United Parcel Service.

Perhaps the story is about Bill Gates or Steve Jobs, each of whom went on to lead the world's largest technology companies. Microsoft has made Gates one of the richest men in the world. While its rival Apple played second fiddle for a good part of its history, Apple has become one of the most highly valued company in the world. Or maybe the story is about Kendra Scott, who started an eponymous billion-dollar jewelry enterprise in her bedroom. On the other side of the world, Jack Ma founded Alibaba, now a global empire, in his apartment.

Long before any of these people were born, Thomas Edison built the beginnings of the corporate behemoth General Electric. It is the same story over and over again. An idea supported by sacrifice and sweat equity bore an amazing outcome. It was merit that not only made these companies but became part of their culture.

As we hear these stories repeatedly throughout our lifetime, they take on a special place in our culture. In Germany, adults tell children, "work hard and you will be rewarded." The phenomenal success of educating children in East Asia is predicated around the same notion of achievement and excellence. The American Dream is synonymous with a hard-working success story. Every group that has immigrated to the United States has had to work hard to achieve. Whatever country you pick, the story is likely similar.

Ask any board of a Fortune 1000 if their company is built on a merito-cratic system, and the answer will be a resounding, "Yes!" Employees get promoted based upon their performance. Hard work and dedication led to the corporate promised land. If this is true, why do we need to develop our leaders on creating an inclusive environment that engages a diverse workforce? After all, our corporate culture is based on meritocracy, right? Those who put in the effort will be rewarded, regardless of their differences.

The answer may be enveloped in another question. Ask that same board if women are inferior to men in the work that needs to be done to make the company successful. In the quarter century we have been consultants to companies around the globe, we have rarely received an affirmative answer to that question. Yet, this answer conflicts with the belief in a culture of meritocracy, as demonstrated by the relative scarcity of women in top corporate positions.

More than half of the labor force is made up of women, and any given Fortune 1000 company will have a workforce of approximately 50 percent women. An educational attainment study done in 2017 showed that women are earning degrees at the same rate as men. Therefore, if women make up half the workforce, are as likely as men to have a degree, and are not inferior in doing the work that makes a company successful, then we need to have a meritocracy reality check.

A 2018 Catalyst Global Census showed that women hold fewer than a quarter (24 percent) of senior roles globally, down from 25 percent in 2017. On another somber note, the census showed that 25 percent of global businesses had no women at all in senior leadership roles. According to a 2018 Pew Research study, the Fortune 500 fared much worse, with fewer than 5 percent of CEO positions held by women. To add one more example of inequity, women held only 11.5 percent of the top-earning positions. Now, how can this be if we have a meritocratic corporate culture? If you are thinking, "Well, this is because women take an off-ramp to have children" or "There isn't enough work–life flexibility," a large body of research on the reasons that women leave companies points in a different direction. The Catalyst Quick Take: Turnover and Retention study found that the two main "push" drivers that cause women to leave their employer are lack of advancement opportunities and lack of respect. The feelings behind these factors are comfort and unconscious preferences for leadership and style.

Work–life balance is inaccurately cited as the main barrier for women; instead the corporate climate is of primary importance in women choosing to stay or leave. Ask yourself why we would need to enact laws that force employers to pay women equally for equal work. In a true meritocracy, your gender would not dictate your pay. The story gets replayed with many other dimensions of difference: ethnicity, education, sexual orientation, gender identity, race, ableness, age, and so on. These dimensions will be expanded upon in a later chapter.

Although we may aspire to have a meritocratic system, the cold hard truth is that it does not yet exist. It does not exist now, nor did it exist fifty years ago, before there was much diversity in the workplace. However, this is probably not a novel concept to you. Have you ever met a manager who made you wonder how he got his position? Does he have the same alma mater as one of the executives? Is he related to a senior executive? Does he look and act like those in power?

If we all agree that our corporate structure is not a true meritocracy, does that fact provide sufficient reason to invest the company's time and hard-earned revenue into developing an inclusive culture? If not, then why are global corporations spending $8 billion a year in this learning endeavor? Some will argue that we live in a litigious society and are in constant fear of being sued. Later in this chapter, we will speak to the legal aspects of diversity and how lack of attention to diversity remains a very real liability. Some of this investment is admittedly tied to legal compliance. However, $8 billion sounds like an awful lot to remain compliant on one aspect of employment law. There must be more to it.

In an interview series on the evolution of diversity and inclusion, we asked chief diversity officers what percentage of corporate development they believe is being driven today by legal compliance. Not one of them gave an answer above 30 percent. If the push for diversity is not driven by a desire to stay out of court, what is it? This question brings us back to why we believe so strongly in a merit-based culture.

Don't we want the best and brightest to be steering our ship? This line of thought argues that when we put the most productive workers in our most critical positions, we maximize corporate value and shareholder return.

However, long-standing barriers prevent meritocracy from becoming a reality. Herein rests the need to invest in opening up channels for a more meritocratic system. The return on this investment can be considerable. A study commissioned by Merrill Lynch analyzed sixty-one publicly traded companies that made *Working Mother* magazine's list of "100 Best Companies." It suggested that companies on the list also provided superior shareholder returns. While the S&P 500 had a strong 89 percent return over three years, companies included on the *Working Mother* list showed an even stronger return of 98 percent. In 2018 *Fortune* magazine published the list of "The Best Workplaces for Diversity." Many of these companies were also top Wall Street performers. These companies beat Standard & Poor's 500 index in three of the prior five years to the report's published date. Anecdotal evidence abounds as well. Frito-Lay enjoys a $100 million revenue stream tied directly to its Hispanic employee resource group. Estée Lauder launched its best-selling fifty-shades product line in direct response to its diversity and inclusion initiatives. The Dora the Explorer brand stems from an attempt to reach the Latino community. It now delivers Nickelodeon $1 billion in royalties and fees annually. Both IBM's Watson and Apple's iPad had diverse groups of leaders on their R&D teams. Cisco credits its ongoing technological innovation to its diverse leadership team. All of these companies invested considerably in creating an inclusive environment to allow merit to prevail.

Your inclusion dividend could be as directly related to D&I investment as the stories above, or it could be more indirect—for example, your dividend could be paid out in the form of improved morale, which increases productivity. When an organization is inclusive, the profits received by shareholders increase. Inclusion can create a surplus, an unexpected gain in productivity or customer engagement. Inclusion creates a tangible advantage in the marketplace.

A Quick History Lesson

Let's first focus on diversity. Very simply put, diversity is the presence of difference. It can be measured, tracked, and recorded. There are self-identifying differences, which are more difficult to put into a spreadsheet, but we will talk about those in a later chapter.

Outside of manual labor, corporations in the United States did not have a diverse workforce for the first century and half after independence. Only white men had high-paying jobs. Men of color were relegated to low-paying and often behind-the-scenes hospitality employment, or to farming-related jobs. Even white men of certain ethnicities, often recent immigrant populations, were blocked from gainful employment. Women of color were almost entirely relegated to domestic worker or agricultural jobs. White women were expected to tend to the home, unless their socioeconomic class required them to work. When they did get jobs in offices, they most likely worked in clerk positions. Their share of these positions was less than 5 percent until the 1930s. The Great Depression made families desperate for household revenue. Desperate times changed the prevailing culture and started to categorize certain jobs as "feminine." By 1940, almost 100 percent of clerk and clerk typists' positions were filled by women, usually white.

As we look at history, we see that times of great need produce the greatest cultural shifts. Both World War I and II opened the doors of employment for women. When WWI ended, those doors shut quickly. However, after WWII it was impossible to fully close them again. WWII also eventually led to the racial integration of the military under President Truman in 1948. It was not until 1964 that President Johnson signed the Civil Rights Act, making major forms of discrimination against African Americans and other racial, ethnic, and religious minorities, as well as women, illegal in and out of the workplace.

These groundbreaking legal changes, however, did not create immediate change. Hiring practices, for example, were still very slanted against women and people of color. Even as more women and people of color applied for a broader range of jobs, increasing the diversity of the candidate pipeline, organizations were slow to expand their hiring of women and people of color beyond their traditional roles. Thus, many workplaces continued to have a severe lack of diversity because the increasing diverse pipeline of candidates was not translating into more inclusive hiring decisions. President Johnson signed an executive order in 1965 that required federal contractors to take "affirmative action" to hire without regard to race, religion, or national origin. Three years later, gender was added to the list.

Diversity in the workplace was not a US-only issue during these times. Reservation in India, a form of affirmative action, created a quota system for certain classes and castes for institutional and government jobs. Britain passed the Equal Pay Act, Sex Discrimination Act, and Race Relations Act successively in the 1970s. The Canadian Human Rights Act, passed in 1977, also extended protections on the basis of gender, disability, and religion. This act paved the way for Canada's "affirmative action" legislation, known as the Employment Equity Act. Similar programs have been implemented in Malaysia, South Africa, and other countries across the globe; including recent examples such as Brazil's race-based affirmative action employment law, passed in 2014.

All of this legislation—and the simple fact that our demographics are trending toward more multicultural societies across the globe, more participation of women in the workplace, and more global companies doing business in many cultures—created greater diversity in large companies; in other words, it created a workplace with more difference. It is not uncommon today for many to equate diversity with legal compliance with all of these legislative acts. When corporations failed to comply with the new laws, they soon faced court-ordered financial penalties.

"Diversity work" in the 1970s and '80s in the United States basically had two components: legal compliance and training—and the training was for the most part about what not to do in order to avoid a lawsuit. Some cutting-edge companies were doing training that focused on interpersonal competence or "valuing" diversity. The attention, again, was mostly on the interpersonal level. When "inclusion" training began, it too was focused at the interpersonal level (i.e., the importance of including other people).

At The Dagoba Group, we define inclusion as a systemic aspiration: the goal is to include everyone, to create a climate that is inclusive, and to create talent acquisition and management processes that are inclusive and fair. In our view, all of this is done not as an add-on, or nice thing to have, but as something essential for maximizing the ability of an organization to meet its mission. In today's global business environment, we see no other way. In today's world, diversity is a given, many major demographic shifts have occurred, and many companies are global, with offices all over the world. Increasingly, these global offices are filled with leadership teams that include expats from the home office combined with local talent. Diversity is already here at certain levels. The challenge is to bring it to all levels. And if you want meritocracy, and you already have diversity, you need inclusion. Meritocracy requires inclusion to work and diversity for fuel. The fuel is in the tank, are you ready to drive?

The Business Case

We will change tenses shortly, from history to the current business case for inclusion. Not only was the US population growing in the twentieth century, the demographics were changing more quickly than anticipated by the general public. As we entered the 1980s, major shifts were being predicted. Among the shifts were:

- An increase in the percentage of the population who are people of color: according to a Pew Population report, non-Hispanic whites will make up less than half (47 percent) of the US population by 2050; Hispanics will grow their share to 29 percent by the same date
- An aging population: the nation's elderly population will more than double in size from 2005 to 2050 as baby boomers begin to retire
- Many more women in the workplace overall, and in higher-level jobs.

A larger percentage of the population composed of minorities meant more and more potential buyers other than white males. As women took on more employment and independence, they were also making more financial decisions.

Smart companies understood there was profit to be made by catering to this growing population. However, a corporate culture that did not welcome diversity within the decision-making process greatly stifled innovation. A company could be "diverse" and still not be inclusive. Numerically, diversity appeared to be working. A closer look at the pool of diversity told a different story. People of color and women were in abundance in entry-level positions, but were largely absent at the higher levels of management.

How did this phenomenon impact profit? If you were trying to market a product to women but did not have women in your marketing, R&D, or sales leadership positions, the corporation was at a huge disadvantage in relating to the target group. As we discussed earlier in this chapter, a culture of inclusion that allows a diverse population to move along all lines of leadership, powers innovation and results in measurable revenue generation.

In addition to the product development realm, the internal workings of the company became an important focus for inclusion efforts. How do you create the dynamics that allow diverse teams to work together effectively? Research indicates that diversity is a high-risk, high-reward proposition. The general view of diverse teams is that they should perform better than homogenous teams because they bring multiple perspectives and ways to approach challenges. One senior manager at a large communications company noted, in describing his experience making gender-diverse teams work together effectively:

> When I observed mostly female teams working together I noticed a different way of working. It was more involving and inclusive, and it had a positive impact on performance. As a new leader I wanted that dynamic on my teams, so over time I was able to create a very gender-diverse leadership team. However, they didn't work together very well at first. I was mystified and then realized that the diversity wasn't enough. I had to do something as a leader to create the right climate.

This insight speaks to the role of inclusion. The research indicates that, in order for diverse teams to work together well and exceed the performance of homogenous teams, the leader needs to create a climate that encourages the full participation of the whole team.

At this point, you can see how a company could be diverse and not inclusive. Can it be the other way around? Technically the answer is "yes" in only one sense. If a company has managed to hire a homogenous group of employees, the internal climate may be such that this group of employees feels engaged and included and is able to largely perform at its best. However, the reality is that demographic changes are making it more difficult to have a homogenous organization. To have a nondiverse organization, except in the rarest case of an industry or function that attracts a largely homogenous group of employees, is neither practical nor possible. Of course, some organizations, via their talent acquisition practices, may severely limit the diversity of those who are hired. Some, via their talent management systems, may also limit the diversity of those who are developed and promoted. Perhaps the homogenous group that is hired and promoted feels included. However, this does not fit our definition of inclusion. Our definition of inclusion goes beyond just how people feel. It includes systems and processes, not just people's individual feelings.

To us and to a growing number of companies it is clear that the most profitable path is to have an organization that is both diverse and inclusive. A corporation can be successful at creating a culture of inclusion, where diverse groups can have not just a seat at the table, but also a full voice in the conversation. This means a focus on creating inclusive systems and practices throughout the entire employee life cycle from recruiting to selection to development and promotion. In chapter 5, where we discuss unconscious bias, we will speak to the unintentional behaviors that create roadblocks for robust and inclusive processes at every point in this life cycle.

Stagnant growth can be a barrier to a flow of entry-level and management candidates. Growth stagnation is the proverbial catch-22. If your growth is limited because of a lack of diversity of thought and innovation, it will be difficult to increase diversity in the pipeline, as the current need for any pipeline is near nonexistent. The idea is to create a healthy flow of a wide variety of employees before you hit a financial stalemate.

Dimensions of Difference

We have been speaking about diversity in the workplace without delineating some of those dimensions of difference in the corporate space. It should be noted that corporations, like people, are manifestations of their culture. Diversity challenges for Tata Consultancy of India may not be the same as those for Germany's Deutsche Bundespost. We'll go into more detail in chapter 7, "Dimensions of Difference."

It is important to capture a working knowledge of each aspect of diversity currently part of the corporate lexicon. There are seven dimensions of difference that are part of the diversity conversation in most corporations: gender, age, sexual orientation, ableness, race, culture/ethnicity and, more recently, gender identity. Other areas where there has been consideration and discussion are veteran status, religion, and socioeconomic class. Gender diversity not only tops the list, it is applicable universally. In an interview with Neddy Perez, former Chief Diversity Officer of Ingersoll Rand, we asked her opinion about the most popular corporate diversity initiative. She said, "In every industry I know, the number one focus is around the development of women. That is both on a US and a global basis. Women are the number one focus in most corporations. Every company that has a D&I focus will have some kind of initiative around women in place." In today's workplace, the subject of age (often referred to as generational diversity) is common as well. Most workforces across the globe include at least three, and often four, distinct generations. Each generation has its own set of experiences, influences, and assumptions about the workplace.

Ethnicity (cultural component) and race (skin color) are not as universally applicable and are sometimes specific to geography. What a corporation in Taiwan considers ethnically and racially diverse will be different from the assumptions for a company in France. As globalization continues though, there is an important race conversation that spans many regions. That conversation is often about the experiences of people of color versus the experiences of whites. In the United States, the race conversation has become more urgent given our broader societal dynamics about race and immigration. Corporations are sometimes at the forefront of the D&I dialogue. Case in point would be the introduction of corporate same sex couple benefits years before same sex marriage was legal. The same is true on the issue of gender identity, as some companies hold the line on inclusive practice even as states pass regressive and restrictive laws against the transgender community.

Gender, age, ethnicity, and race are the four dimensions of difference most often reported. Self-identifying areas of diversity, such as veteran status, sexual orientation, or certain forms of disability, are much harder to track and more difficult to apply globally. These are aspects of diversity that an employee or candidate would need to self-disclose. The ability and the perceived or actual need to address certain issues vary regionally and globally. For example, efforts to increase diversity by hiring US veterans are typically not a concern for a recruiter in Poland. Lesbian, gay, or bisexual individuals have an added roadblock in some countries due to discriminatory laws and practices. Definitions of disability are also up for debate across borders as well as within organizations.

As we grow as a global business society, we will not only see more of what we have in common, but also the value of our differences. Actions to increase diversity are a starting point, but full empowerment and inclusion must be the goal.

If the intent is to have the most productive and effective organization, then the goal of a diverse, inclusive workplace is a meritocracy. Although diversity and inclusion can exist independently of each other, a true meritocracy requires a solid D&I foundation. We define meritocracy as a system in which rewards are based on an individual's performance and demonstrated ability.

The word "rewards" has any number of connotations in this context. Being contacted for an interview could be seen as a reward. In the same vein, hiring is a reward. Too often, rewards are associated only with the compensation area. Of course, raises and bonuses are an integral aspect of the reward system. Promotions, project assignments, expanded responsibilities, and recognition are also part of the reward structure.

A meritocracy looks beyond an affinity one candidate has with the hiring manager or the project manager's propensity to "work better with generation X engineers." The notion of a meritocracy can admittedly be very intimidating to those who rose to the top through connections rather than based on their performance. It is also human nature to gravitate toward those who most resemble us. Looking at the leadership of many companies today, you can find a strong sense of homogeneity, the quality of being similar or comparable.

The very first impression is appearance. Are leaders mostly of one gender? Of one race? Of one generation? Other commonalities may not be as apparent. Do they have alma maters in common? Are they the same sexual orientation? Do they live in the same area of town? Belong to the same clubs? Do they share a common working background? Did they tend to be recruited from a particular area of the company? The list can be lengthy, but you often find less and less diversity within small and large groups as you move up in the management ranks or to higher-paying professions.

Challenges to Creating Inclusion

There are some very real challenges to creating a true meritocratic system, particularly in two common business types: family-owned businesses and large corporations.

1. **Family-owned businesses:** How meritocratic can a family-owned business become? Your unconscious bias may have just set in when the words "family owned" were used. This term is typically connected with small enterprises like farms, restaurants, dry cleaners, and the like. Did you think of the largest employers in the world? The Walton family still owns a controlling share in Walmart. As of the writing of this book, the Ford family also maintains a controlling share of Ford Motor Company. Those two companies together employ close to two million people. Samsung, LG Group, Cargill, Cathay Life Insurance Co., Tyson Foods, and Ikea are just a few more examples of multibillion-dollar family-controlled corporations.

Family-owned/controlled businesses can discover that creating a meritocratic system is more difficult because of a lack of diversity in senior management. What is more homogeneous than a family? Frequently the same culture, background, race, ethnicity, etc. If meritocracy sits on a foundation of diversity and inclusion, lack of strength in one of these areas can be analogous to a chair with one leg shorter than the others: the tendency is to lean in a particular direction.

Does this mean a family business cannot be meritocratic? It is not impossible, but it does require a far higher degree of self-awareness and diligence. Imagine the difficulty of choosing between your own nephew, who may not be the best fit for the position, and an unrelated candidate who has the strengths to move the company forward. Our altruistic selves tell us we would pick the stronger candidate because that would be the best choice for the company. However, when it comes down to the actual choice, hiring managers who have not developed an acute self-awareness would pick the nephew every time. After all, it is a family business, right?

2. **Large corporations:** The higher the number of employees, the more likely we will naturally move toward those who are like us because

there is a measure of familiarity and safety with populations you know. This phenomenon can be readily seen when large groups of people of like origins immigrate to a country. For many reasons, they create ghettos, geographical areas dominated by particular ethnic groups. In any large city in the United States one can find a Chinatown or Little Italy or the gay neighborhood. The same is true for "insider" groups, such as whites, or the upper classes, who tend to cluster. When we are in large groups, we unconsciously seek out likeness as a means of support and comfort. These ghettos result from both discriminatory practices and personal choice. It is difficult to ascertain which is governing the creation of ghettos, however there is little doubt of the role of bias and discrimination, at least historically. An interesting challenge, which we will cover in much greater detail later, is the role that power plays in the way the dynamic of ghettoization is understood. When minority (lower power) groups cluster, it is noticed and remarked upon. When majority (higher power) groups cluster it is often not noticed, at least by the majority group(s). In one of our Inclusive Leadership sessions, a participant remarked that all the people of color would group together at large corporate events. He never realized that all the white men and women were doing the same thing until he was challenged to view it from another perspective. Additionally, the impact of this "clustering," or ghettoization, is very different, as it limits minority groups while expanding access for majority groups.

Like begets like. Ask any company that gains more than 30 percent of its employees through referrals whether it has an issue with creating diverse teams. Departments with a higher degree of employee referrals have less heterogeneity. When there is a propensity to form similar groups in large crowds, processes that feed the growth of those crowds need greater attention in order for a healthy and diverse population to exist. In chapter 9, "Change Strategies for Creating Inclusion," we speak to methods that help enhance not only the diversity but also the inclusion in large corporations.

Other Inclusion Hurdles

We spoke briefly about the challenges for both family-owned and large corporations. Does this mean if you are a nonfamily-owned small-to medium-sized business, meritocracy is guaranteed? No. There are still multiple hurdles to overcome.

Before we can create a work environment where everyone is valued, we need to inventory the current organization. This inventory should be taken with awareness of three levels: individual, group, and system. We will go into greater depth on these areas in the "Framing a Sustainable Inclusion Initiative" chapter. For now, it is sufficient to know that the entire organization (system) is made up of many groups, based on social identity (e.g., age, ableness, culture, gender, race, sexual orientation) and working groups (e.g., subsidiaries, departments, teams). Each group is either made up of other groups or, in its lowest level, consists of employees (individuals).

Inclusion can be furthered or hindered at every level. Understanding the level of bias or inclusion at all three levels will give the corporation greater clarity about areas of opportunity. Systems contain processes, culture, and "tradition," which may need to be adjusted to open a wider pipeline of candidates to be hired and candidates for promotion. Patterns of experience based on group identity give strong clues about barriers to inclusion. Team culture can often be set by management, and it can be intentionally inclusive or unintentionally exclusive. Allowing management to become more aware of their impact on the group as a whole and on individual employees provides a road map for improvement.

Awareness on an individual level comes from skilled consultation and development. A manager does not wake up one morning and become perfectly self-aware. As mentioned earlier in this chapter, corporations are spending billions of dollars annually to make their workforces more diverse and their environments more inclusive. The great bulk of this investment is made in leadership development to help alleviate three major bottlenecks to a merit-based system: candidate acquisition, hiring, and talent management.

Diversity begins with reaching a wide range of talent, but candidate acquisition is fraught with unintentional narrowing of reach. For example, companies select specific universities from which to recruit while ignoring all the others. Not only does this narrow educational diversity, it may also affect other areas of difference. Perhaps those universities have a very low African American population. Or maybe they attract individuals of only a certain economic class because of their tuition level. The university itself could have career counselors who hold unconscious biases and tend to send only a certain group of individuals to career events.

Corporations allow "tradition" to put them in a rut of advertising in the same media for years or of seeking talent only from within the industry. In a Dagoba Group interview, Lorie Valle-Yanez, Chief Diversity Officer for MassMutual Financial Group, spoke to this point when she said, "For this industry [insurance], it is very challenging. It has been around for a long time and is very conservative and somewhat insular. We end up stealing the same talent from each other. It is an industry issue." When corporations fail to continually adjust their nets or find different pools, they end up getting the same fish over and over again.

A lot of time and investment goes into creating a diverse pipeline of candidates. Quality is often seen as filtered quantity. The filter is the next major challenge. Candidates must pass muster with a very busy recruiter before meeting the hiring manager's expectations. This is a common area where unconscious bias plays a strong role. A series of studies over the last fifteen years, including a landmark 2004 study conducted by MIT and University of Chicago showed a strong bias in the recruitment process with regard to applicant names. In the MIT study, researchers sent 5,000 résumés to 1,250 employers. The résumés of highly skilled individuals were identical with the exception of the name: on one résumé, researchers put a "black-sounding" name and on the other a "white-sounding" name. Candidates with white-sounding names received 50 percent more callbacks than those with black-sounding names. More recent studies, in the United States and globally, have found similar results related to other racial groups, gender, religious affiliation, and sexual orientation. In Canada, a study found a bias toward Asian names while in Europe the bias was toward Middle Eastern names.

We could look at this from purely a return-on-investment view. If a company is spending $100,000 to advertise its open positions, but because of poor filtering only 50 percent of qualified candidates are getting through, it is wasting $50,000. All of this money and time was spent to reach a diverse audience, only to have the effort stopped short during the recruiting process. In our "Reducing Unconscious Bias in Interviewing and Selection" workshop, we take recruiters and hiring managers through every step of the hiring process to identify potential areas of bias. Raising awareness of these structures helps to adjust the filter so that all qualified candidates pass through. You get your $100,000-worth of candidates.

Hiring a diverse set of employees is one thing, keeping them is another. The old adage, "Employees leave managers, not companies," has a lot of truth to it. If an employee does not feel welcomed to be her full self, it will not be long before she takes her talent to another organization, one that will accommodate her. Even during the worst years of our most recent global recession, there were still millions of jobs unfilled.

Critical skilled positions, such as nurse, engineer, and developer, are vital to the success of corporations seeking to be on the cutting edge of their field. Only one company can be the highest paying in the industry. Money is not a long-term employee retention value. Creating a corporate culture where employees feel valued and part of a team is a longer-term retention strategy. Corporations can only create that place when they develop the skill sets of their leaders and associates.

Companies that have made a true commitment to creating a diverse and inclusive culture will start development at the senior executive level. Senior executives are more insulated from the working environment than most employees, so they possess the greatest need to become aware of how inclusion can create greater value for the company. The behavior of those at the chief officer level tends to be replicated down through the ranks. Reinforcing inclusive behavior at mid- and lower-management levels helps to cement a culture in which good intention results in a positive impact.

Development is not a one-time action. Try to teach someone how to use advance features of Microsoft Excel, or any complex skill or concept, with just a one-time course. Learners need to practice new skills over and over again and consult reference guides; often, they require refresher courses. Excel is a defined system with limits. Human behavior is not so defined and can feel quite limitless. Over the past few years, we have read many articles asserting that diversity and inclusion training does not work. Some expect that attending one workshop will erase decades of learned behavior. Repeated leadership development in many different forms is required if behavioral change is to take hold. Our clients build sustainment plans to continue the learning well beyond the leadership development course. Participating in employee resource groups and engaging in continual development are two very important behavioral change efforts. This book is certainly one of those forms, so you are on your way.

We began this story with some entrepreneurs in their garages starting amazing corporations. Each one of these founders would tell you they could not have done it alone or with the help only of people exactly like themselves. All benefited greatly from a diversity of talent and thought. Holding onto a goal of creating a meritocratic system, they have all invested heavily in building diverse talent pipelines and developing their corporate leadership. The return on investment continues to be astounding, and in our increasingly diverse societies, the best is yet to come.

In this chapter, we introduced three key terms: meritocracy, diversity, and inclusion, and we discussed briefly the history of diversity in the workplace and how the business case drives inclusion. We also presented some typical challenges to inclusion and meritocracy. Finally, we itemized the dimensions of difference so you could begin to appreciate those topical areas, which we'll discuss later. Below are some takeaways you should hold onto as you read further.

Takeaways

- ✓ Diversity is a measure of difference.
- ✓ Inclusion is the extent to which diverse groups have a seat at the table and are able to bring their best contributions.
- ✓ Diversity and inclusion can exist independently of each other; however, this is increasingly difficult to do.
- ✓ Meritocracy is a system in which rewards and opportunities are based on an individual's performance and demonstrated ability.
- ✓ Meritocracy requires both inclusion to work and diversity for fuel.
- ✓ There are challenges to meritocracy, diversity, and inclusion that are inherent to corporate structures and processes.
- ✓ The vast majority of barriers to meritocracy are unintentional and/ or unconscious.
- ✓ There are seven major dimensions of difference in today's corporate focus: gender, sexual orientation, culture/ethnicity, race, age, ableness, and, most recently, gender identity. There are many more emerging topics.

✓ Inclusion today is focused on the business case—on how an inclusive environment yields better results for the company.

✓ There are three levels of system to be addressed to create an inclusive culture in an organization: individual, group, and organization.

✓ An effectively implemented D&I strategy will return dividends in many different forms.

Discussion Point

InfoXTR Computer is a Fortune 1000 public company that takes pride in being on the bleeding edge of innovation. It has invested heavily in an employer brand that talks about a meritocratic culture and promotion from within. The company has never had a layoff. "Employees who put in their time get rewarded," is the company's guiding philosophy. InfoXTR values reliability and loyalty. Because of its emphasis on loyalty, the company has practically no turnover in executive positions. Retention levels are very high at director level and above.

InfoXTR is developing a new operating system based on a unique programming language. It has a director-level spot open to lead this new R&D offshoot. This position is considered one of those jobs everybody dreams will open up. Needless to say, InfoXTR received many internal expressions of interest. Because there was so much interest internally, the company decided not to post the position externally.

After many interviews, the search team narrowed the choices to two individuals. Chris, who has been with InfoXTR for the past twenty years, has taken on many tough assignments, has moved several times for the company, and has been on the "waiting list" for a promotion for a couple of years now. Chris is familiar with the language but has not worked with it directly.

The other candidate, Raj, started with the company two years ago. Raj is one of the primary contributors in building this new programming language. He joined the company because of its innovation and "promotion from within" branding.

The new OS could be a real game changer for the industry. Some of InfoXTR's products have gotten dusty, and there are a lot of upstart competitors entering the market.

Given the story above, how would you answer the following questions?

♦ Who should get the position? Why?

♦ What is your guess on the state of meritocracy at InfoXTR? Why?

♦ If you were going to paint a picture of diversity for InfoXTR, what would it look like?

♦ Does an "innovation" brand work well with a "promotion from within" brand? How do you see these two brands impacting inclusion or diversity?

♦ If you were hired as a talent acquisition and management consultant for InfoXTR, would you change anything? Why or why not?

2

The Business Case
for Inclusion

Companies are in business, first and foremost, to make a profit. Profits keep the lights on and the employees paid, and they also allow companies to invest in their people and communities. Investments made within the corporate walls need to accomplish at least one of two things: reduce expenses or increase revenues. The business case is the story behind reaching one or hopefully both of these goals. The margin of return needs to be a ratio greater than 1:1. Profit is not made if every dollar spent only brings in a dollar. The same is essentially true for nonprofit entities; while not-for-profits aren't looking for profit, they are most certainly looking to achieve a mission, and for that they need funds in addition to the amount it takes to keep the organization running. Whether you call it a business case or a mission-driven rationale, every diversity and inclusion effort needs to be directly connected to the organization's purpose.

Workforce inclusion efforts and demographic trends have created a more diverse workplace. In the 1980s we began hearing about these changes via the report *Workforce 2000*. This demographic shift is no longer an event to plan for. It has arrived. Though diversity is slower to increase in the leadership ranks, there is clearly greater diversity among those in management positions. Diversity in management is greater almost across the board, as women and people of color have taken on more and more of these roles. There is greater cultural diversity as well. Openly LGBT (lesbian, gay, bisexual, or transgender) people are now more common in management. Agewise, while the cohort of generation Y employees are about to begin their careers, millennials are joining generation Xers and baby boomers in management and leadership positions even as many baby boomers are retiring or changing the way they work. This increasingly diverse set of leaders and decision makers is present in your organization, and also in your current or potential client and customer organizations.

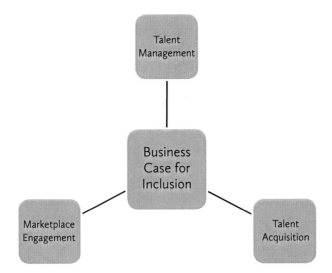

FIGURE 2-1 The Business Case for Inclusion

Three Key Areas for Inclusion

In this chapter, we will discuss the business case with regard to three key areas: talent management, talent acquisition, and marketplace engagement. These areas stem from two vantage points: internal dynamics and external relationships. Internally, the focus is on attracting, retaining, and developing staff. More specifically, the emphasis is on these factors:

- Talent acquisition: Are we accessing a broad employment pool and does our brand attract a diverse set of potential employees?
- Talent development: Are we creating conditions and opportunities that tap the talent of a diverse workforce?
- Employee engagement: Do we inclusively engage our diverse workforce? Do our employees feel good about the company and are they able to bring their best contributions? Are we retaining high-potential employees?
- Workplace climate: Does the day-to-day environment promote inclusion and success? Does our culture promote teamwork and innovation?

We most often think about D&I in the context of the workforce. Attracting, retaining, and developing the best and brightest talent are pivotal to a healthy, profit-driven organization. Less common, and at least as important, is applying inclusion tactics to attracting, retaining, and developing clients or customers. After all, clients and customers are people, not just corporate entities. To fully explore the business case for inclusion, we need to talk about the challenges and opportunities within the marketplace, more specifically:

- Consumer brand: Is our brand inclusive? Do we attract a consumer base that is diverse?
- Products and services: In the business-to-consumer space, do our products reflect the needs of an increasingly diverse and ever-changing marketplace? Are we attracting and retaining a workforce that will drive industry-leading innovation?

- Client engagement: In the business-to-business space, how effectively do we build our relationships with our clients? Do we engage them inclusively? Do we use our diversity and theirs to deepen and broaden client relationships?

The following is a true story of a business that had every opportunity to become a dot-com superstar valued in the billions. We will call this company RecruitXMe.com and we'll call the employee Francis.

In the early 2000s, Francis joined the budding start-up online site RecruitXMe.com. Like most dot-coms, the company was fast paced and dynamic. It had just acquired a competitor, and the competitor's name-plate was still on the New York office door when Francis began his first day in a sales role. The company was fighting for market share against the industry behemoth, so the name of the game was new client acquisition, and fast. The approach was highly transactional, without much energy invested in developing a relationship. Sales reps received bonuses based on the number of new accounts they opened.

This somewhat mechanical approach to gaining new client accounts was replicated in the candidate acquisition approach. As the company grew market share, it needed to hire sales reps and customer service reps quickly. Talent acquisition was very transactional. Recruiters were rewarded for meeting the numbers. There was no established metric or reward for quality of hire. Management, which for the most part grew from the sales ranks, was not provided leadership development.

In just a few years, the number of clients grew exponentially, until there were thousands. The number of employees at RecruitXMe.com went from a few hundred to more than a thousand. The parallel did not stop there. At the start of each year, the company had a sales kickoff event, with all hands on deck. After Francis's first year, a trend began to appear. Coworkers who sat to the left and right of him at the beginning of the year were, more often than not, gone the following year. Client attrition was also rising. The declining client renewal rate showed up in reports and generated a whole lot of programs designed to stem the tide. And, although employee turnover showed up on HR reports, the company did not invest much in retaining good employees. Programs to train managers on how to manage or to develop executive leadership were not put on the table.

During a break at the 2010 kickoff, Francis stood up to stretch and suddenly realized something interesting as he gazed around the auditorium at hundreds of his fellow sales colleagues. First, everyone was white. Yes, every single person in that auditorium was white. This event included sales reps from all the offices, from Houston to New York to Los Angeles. He also noticed that almost all of them were male and, as far as he knew, straight. A lover of probability problems, Francis asked himself, "What are the odds that an organization in such great need of employees in major metropolitan areas is sourcing only white straight males?"

It was not until Francis took on a role at RecruitXMe.com corporate headquarters that he found a striking echo. Because his job involved better reaching decision makers within their targeted buying audience, he wanted to understand who they were currently engaging. He sent a study to every sales rep in each office, asking about the demographics of their top ten accounts. Because demographics were not collected within the CRM program, Francis contacted each rep by phone to discuss the age, gender, and race of the decision makers at top clients. After the first twenty surveys, it became clear there were a lot of commonalities between the sales reps and the decision makers. The typical user of the service was a recruiter, so at first it seemed that perhaps the clients simply fit the stereotype of a person who works in a corporate recruiting department.

However, the commonalities changed with the demographic profile of the sales rep. At the time, 99 percent of the sales reps were non-Hispanic white, so the racial demographic was shared by all reps. The male reps, interestingly, had a much higher number of male clients than the female reps did. The 1 percent of reps who were not white, had a much higher percentage of non-white clients. The link to common ground was distinct.

The tendency to favor those with shared characteristics was also clear within the workplace: straight, white, male managers were hiring straight, white, male reps. When an office took on a female manager, the percentage of female reps soared.

When an economic downturn hit, clients either dramatically reduced their need or left in droves. They were not simply abandoning the online recruitment industry, they were streamlining their vendors of choice. Because there was no relationship, clients chose vendors on perception and pricing alone. On more than one occasion, managers discovered that reps were sending renewal contracts with steep increases via email, without ever meeting the client. The reps had been hired in a transactional manner, were not developed beyond training in sales methodology, and were being managed by reports that required a set number of proposals out the door per week. In a couple of years, hundreds of millions of dollars in annual business flew out the door. Other upstarts in the industry were picking up steam, and fast.

The CEO of RecruitXMe.com instituted corporate innovation contests, but the innovation entries were simply not that innovative. The entries that made it to the final round were chosen by mid-to senior-level managers. Time and again, the innovations selected sapped the company of resources without adding to the bottom line. The CEO was asking a homogeneous management group that had hired a homogenous sales force to be innovative; to think differently while being surrounded by sameness. Yet, it seemed surprising to them that every year the idea chosen provided negative value. One of the ideas even opened up the company to liability.

Although the company almost halved its revenue base, shed most of its best-performing sales reps, and has yet to introduce an industry-changing innovation, the retained senior management has become more homogeneous: white, straight men. A group of senior executives who graduated from the same university continue to get rewarded. Up to the day the company was acquired, the senior management team strongly believed its culture was a meritocracy. In today's world, how can an organization with such a homogenous leadership team and sales force be a meritocracy? How will this company possibly be able to innovate and lead in its industry? The company did not allow employee affinity groups to form because it thought the practice was exclusionary. These groups of employees coalescing around such issues as race, gender, sexual orientation, age, disability status, and so on might have helped to increase inclusion inside the company. They might have developed innovative ideas. Instead, the inclusion initiative was to put global holidays on the corporate calendar.

The innovative approach to client relationship building was to create a series of golfing events at expensive resorts. Not surprisingly, more than 90 percent of the clients who attended these events were white, straight, and male. The company never regained its peak revenue achievements, while the upstarts have surpassed them. The few minority employees who did eventually get hired and who moved into management have left the company. Even the company's marketing campaigns have lost innovation; it resorted to its original commercial scheme. It was finally acquired for less than half its former value.

This company's example embodies the core questions of the internal and external business case for inclusion that we described earlier. Inclusive employee engagement and diverse talent acquisition are tied directly into client engagement and leading the marketplace. You can't separate the level of engagement of an increasingly diverse workforce from the level of engagement you have with your customers.

The business case for diversity is rooted in anecdotal evidence of revenue-producing results tied to specific D&I initiatives. What happens to a company when there is a lack of inclusion or diversity is not part of the discussion; that is not a story we often hear. Could a more inclusive, diverse employee base have helped RecruitXMe weather the economic storm? Would it have generated a more innovative culture? Would allowing employee resource groups to form have made any difference? Did the company's homogeneous workforce have an impact on its client base or were the commonalities simply coincidence?

When to Invest in Inclusion Development

When revenue is growing fast and furious, it is easy for a company to overlook issues of inclusion. Don't fix what is not broken, right? When the company hits a wall, it is easy to maintain the status quo, failing to commit resources to teach managers how to create an inclusive environment. Who has the time or the money to take managers out of the field so that they can learn to change their behavior? After all, they need to focus 100 percent on keeping the business afloat. So, if it is not the time to develop inclusive leadership when the company is doing well and it's not the time when the company is performing poorly, when is it time?

We think that the right time is "now and always." That is because diversity and inclusion are impacting your company right now. In the past they were seen as separate from the mainstream of the company's business, or they were seen as a potential legal liability and compliance issue. Either that or they were viewed as something good to do if there was enough time and money. However, it is now clear that the ability to create an inclusive organization is directly tied to an organization's success, whether looking from the inside, as an employee trying to build a successful career, or from the outside as a potential employee, customer, or stakeholder. Earlier we discussed how a business case should provide at least one of two things: reduced expenses or increased revenue. In other words, they need to provide increased value to the company. We are going to look more closely at both the internal and external factors in this value proposition. The key external factors include: company brand, market positioning, and customer engagement. The key internal factors include: employee acquisition, employee retention, productivity, and innovation.

The Internal Business Case

SHRM Human Capital Benchmarking studies have placed the cost per hire of a new employee at $4,129, as of 2018. This includes all forms of hiring, from referrals to outsourced staffing. The average agency placement fee is 15 to 20 percent of annual salary for lower-level employees and 25 to 30 percent for senior management. Depending on your firm's reliance on outside agencies, your cost per hire could be dramatically higher than the study's findings. Looking at an aggregated number, companies spent US $3.5 billion on recruitment advertising alone in 2009. In case most of us have wiped that year out of our financial minds, it was the depth of the economic recession. The 2017 *Forbes* article "Google for Jobs" places the global recruitment spend at $200 billion.

Needless to say, even in a down economy the cost of employee acquisition can take a sizeable bite out of profits. It may seem like a bit of a paradox that companies needed to spend so much to find talent when unemployment exceeded 9 percent nationally. Simply typing "talent shortage" into Google's search engine will supply you with the reason: articles on the shortage of oil and gas engineers, nurses, and talent skilled in Linux are just a few of those that will show up in your search results.

As our economy becomes more advanced and specialized, there is an unmet need for candidates with particular skill sets. The Korn Ferry Institute predicts that there will be a global talent shortage of more than 85 million workers by 2030. Additionally, Towers Watson, HR consultants, found that more than 80 percent of companies operating in fast-growth economies and 65 percent of global companies are currently having problems finding employees with desired skill sets. Complicating this issue is the beginning of the baby boomer generation reaching retirement age. AARP notes that by 2030, for the first time in US history, there will be more people over age sixty-five than there are children. Fewer workers in the labor pool and a skill demand higher than supply will require companies to expand their talent pools.

Not having an inclusive approach to the talent pool can deny the company the valuable skilled workers needed for a profitable future. Open positions have direct opportunity costs, some of which are easier to calculate than others. For example, an open sales position that is expected to generate $30,000 in monthly invoicing means a loss of $1,000 per day for every day it is unfilled. Other unfilled positions, such as engineer, could lead to a slower rollout of goods and services, opening the company up to a competitive loss. The dividend is on the flip side: filling these positions means higher revenue and market share potential. If a company continuously fishes for talent from the same pond, supply will eventually run out. Furthermore, if it does not create an inclusive, welcoming environment, the chances of needed talent agreeing to employment decrease rapidly. What is your company's brand in the employment market? Do a number of diverse groups think of your company as a good place to work? Do you have an employment edge on your competitors?

Acquiring talent is only the start of the D&I job. New talent is not an asset if these employees are not productive or if they separate early from the company. The loss of an employee has been estimated to cost up to two and a half times salary. Factors that add into this cost are the acquisition costs mentioned above, training, and lost productivity, not only while the position is open but also during the employee's waning period. Employee retention is the next vital and logical step after talent is hired.

The business case for employee retention is fairly straightforward for the expenses noted. The revenue potential can be a little more subjective, but is commonly detailed on annual reports. For example, Apple enjoys approximately $1.9 million in revenue per employee, while Walmart comes in at $51,000, Amazon at $101,000, and Microsoft at $973,000. The energy industry can see an average revenue per employee in the millions. Looking at these reported numbers, one can calculate the impact of retaining quality talent. Using Microsoft's stats, every day of retention equals an additional $3,800 to the company's top line. In the business-to-business world, where client relationships are king, it is expensive to lose talent, especially when the client may follow the separated employee to her next employer.

When work environments are more welcoming and inclusive, companies enjoy greater retention rates of critical revenue-positive employees. The Level Playing Field Institute did a large and groundbreaking study (Corporate Leavers Survey 2007) that estimated US corporations lose more than $60 billion annually when work environments are not inclusive. The study looked at seventeen hundred leaders who had voluntarily left their employers, and found that 34 percent of people of color would have stayed if the company had a more inclusive management team. The study was updated in 2017 to focus specifically on the tech industry, and discovered that tech companies are losing $16 billion annually because of to their workplace culture. In a public case study, Nextel was able to directly link a 2 percent decrease in turnover to diversity and inclusion training.

Retention efforts focus not only on keeping the best talent, but also on making sure that they are productive. Productivity per employee is a common measure of corporate value by shareholders. Corporations with highly productive employees are valued more than their competition. Cumulative Gallup Workplace Studies uncovered a 22 percent increase in productivity at companies that are effective at creating inclusion when compared with those that are not.

Again, productivity is a common corporate measurement of success. A working D&I strategy not only helps talent acquisition and employee retention, it also creates an environment where employees are more productive. Common sense says that if someone feels good about where he works, he works better. But all of us have, at one time or another, not felt like part of the team. With hindsight, we can easily see it was not the most productive time of our work life.

A highly engaged employee pool is more likely to push the envelope in innovation as well. In a 2011 study, Donald Fan, Senior Director of Diversity at Walmart, found a direct link between diversity and innovation. In his published findings in the August 2011 *Diversity Inc.* magazine, he notes, "While business lore tends to link innovation with a creative drive that is exclusive to the top and brightest talent, true innovation thrives in an inclusive culture that values diverse ideas, leverages unique perspectives and invites everyone to achieve collaborative breakthroughs across the entire organization."

A 2018 McKinsey study found that companies with more gender-diverse executive teams (those companies that placed in the top 25 percent) were 15 percent more likely to have above-average profitability than those with the least gender-diverse teams (those companies in the bottom 25 percent). Rosalind Hudnell, Director of Global Diversity and Inclusion at Intel, remarked, "We have a vast amount of diversity that comes into work every day to build technology that plays out around the world. You can't be successful on a global stage without it."

If the above data points shed any light on the RecruitXMe story, lack of diversity and inclusion may have been contributing factors to the company's lack of market-leading innovation. If we simply take a step back and reexamine our earlier definition of diversity as "the presence of difference," we do not need to take a big leap to see how difference can lead to innovation. Innovation can be basically defined as the introduction of something new. The status quo is commonly seen as the opposite of innovation. In keeping with this line of thought, maintaining sameness (homogeneity) in our teams is unlikely to inspire something new.

Teamwork is central in this equation. More and more of the day-to-day work done in large companies is performed by teams. Increasingly diverse teams represent a huge opportunity, but also a challenge. Most leaders think that a diverse team is a good thing: it means that challenges will be looked at from multiple perspectives, leading to a better result. In fact, a Columbia Business School study of individuals engaged in a trading simulation found that the ethnically diverse teams substantially outperformed the homogenous teams. However, a diverse team does not magically drive innovation. The Columbia study found that being part of a diverse team made individuals think harder. Many of us have been selected to be on teams where the leader was not really looking for input, or where only a few voices were considered. Innovation requires an inclusive approach that welcomes input and openly considers ideas from all sources. Research shows that, when leaders create an inclusive climate on their teams, diverse teams will overperform. On the flip side, under a leader who is not inclusive, diverse teams underperform. The critical factor, as is so often the case, is leadership.

A leader has to be proactive and intentional in creating conditions that encourage a diverse team to overperform. It is important to note that, under certain conditions, homogenous teams outperform diverse teams. This tends to happen with tasks that are not complex and don't require creativity and innovation. How much of the work in your organization is simple and cannot be improved with innovation? At the heart of this conundrum is creating an inclusive team climate, one that engages all of the members of a team. Companies that require every team to be made up of a "diverse" set of individuals but that do not develop group leaders to create an inclusive environment will achieve their diversity numbers goals, but not the overall objective of growing the business or fostering innovation.

There is no mystical pixie dust that comes with a diverse group. If the focus is simply on meeting numbers in employee acquisition or team demographics, then the goal of an engaged, highly productive team that drives business success will be lost in the process. As with any business case, there needs to be a strategic approach to achieve the desired results. It is not uncommon that the corporate business case for diversity and inclusion falls short on the inclusion component. This holistic concept is better understood in successful Marketing and Sales departments where an advertising campaign is teamed up with a sales strategy. Each step of the sales process is aligned with marketing and paired with several metrics to determine success along the way. The same thing is true with diversity and inclusion.

The External Business Case

We have just used a sales analogy, so this is a good time to transition from the internal business case focus to the external D&I approach. As our changing demographics and civil rights movements continue to create a much more diverse pool of decision makers, many companies, especially business-to-consumer companies, have decided that they need to change the way they communicate with their current and future target audience.

The simple approach—what the Nobel Prize-winning economist Daniel Kahneman might call the System 1 approach in his book ***Thinking Fast and Slow***—is to use "mirroring." A System 1 decision-making process is one that is quick and relies mostly on intuition. Have you heard in your place of business that your company wants to "mirror" its target audience? On a basic level (and often it does not go beyond this level), this is a numbers game that involves matching the percentage of minorities in the employee population to those in the customer base. If the customer base is 20 percent Asian, mirroring that audience means that approximately 20 percent of the employees in customer-facing positions are Asian.

Mirroring can be an unfulfilling numbers game that creates more problems than it solves. First, it can be difficult to place such a recruitment burden on your hiring team if the company has no real effort to create an environment that attracts a diverse group of candidates. All sorts of roadblocks, from screening and selection to onboarding and career-pathing, will exist if there is no concerted strategic inclusion effort. Mirroring can be an example where the intent does not match the impact. And the impact can be felt at five distinct phases of the customer relationship process.

RADIX

At The Dagoba Group, we have helped clients leverage their internal inclusion efforts to strengthen their client relationships in the cycle we call RADIX™. A radix is the root of a plant. It helps the plant stay grounded and acquire nutrition, and it provides foundational support. Our RADIX model provides the same benefit to your external revenue-producing clients. The business case for inclusion is extremely visible and easily measured when applied externally.

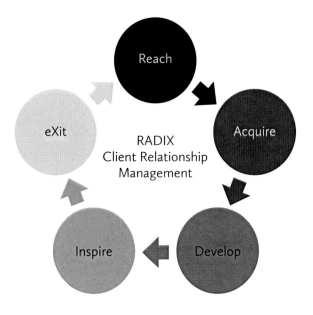

FIGURE 2-2 RADIX Model

You probably guessed correctly that each letter of the model RADIX refers to a stage of the sales process. We start with the Reach—this is the pre-acquisition phase of soliciting potential customers, where there are introductory conversations. Next, we move to Acquire—this stage is considered by many sales teams to be the most critical and celebrated phase of transitioning a potential customer to a signed client. After the client is acquired, there is a need to Develop—at this point, your efforts are focused on fulfilling the pre-acquisition promises and expanding your service footprint. After the honeymoon ends, client relationships often move to the status quo bucket, which requires you to Inspire— it's the time in the relationship where innovation and providing value that goes beyond what was promised play a major role in growing the client and fending off competition. Unfortunately, due to reasons that may or may not be controllable, a client may move to eXit the rela- tionship—this is where managing the separation can help aid in future reacquisition. Yes, we know we cheated with the last word by having the letter in the middle, but how many usable words start with an "X"?

Reach

It is in the Reach stage that companies often start and stop their D&I client efforts. Marketing sees a change in customer demographics, so they include images of the increased demographic in advertising. Think of Pepsi and its "Next Generation" commercials. Pepsi knew the Coke audience was getting older and thought it could carve out market share by closely tying the Pepsi brand to a younger age group. You may have noticed quite an increase of non-whites in consumer-focused advertising. Understanding they were not fully resonating with their growing clientele, consumer-focused companies like McDonald's, Ford, and Gillette greatly increased the number of minority actors in their commercials. They also started to change product lines to better reflect the needs of different demographic groups. Cosmetic companies expanded their lines to include more Latina- and African American–targeted beauty products as they saw the purchasing power of this clientele expand.

Marketing can often miss the mark with the Reach when it does not have a diverse team to draw upon or does not look fully at all of the communication points. This may be what happened to H&M, the trendy department store, which featured all blonde mannequins in its Thirty-Fourth Street store and all brunettes in its Harlem store. Now, marketing was probably trying to "mirror" the demographic they saw as the target population in each area. Unfortunately for them, this was more of an exclusive approach than an inclusive one. Less than half of the population of New York City is white, so why would the company purposefully put only white mannequins in its most customer-facing area (the front window) in its trendy Thirty-Fourth Street location? In 2018, H&M was in the spotlight again with an advertisement image of a black child with a sweatshirt that said, "Coolest Monkey in the Jungle." We strongly believe H&M did not consciously intend to exclude or offend, but like all humans, decision makers at the company may have had an unconscious bias that was not challenged. In both instances, considerable resources had to be diverted to correct the PR damage.

Having fully diverse representation on the team is important. It does not mean you only put African Americans in areas where the company believes the majority of customers will be African American. Nor does it mean that Avon should recruit only women; as a matter of fact, some of the highest-producing cosmetic sales representatives are male. Companies that create diverse teams that include representation of the target market, but which are also inclusive of the entire market, see the best results from their efforts. We mentioned that companies often start and end with this external-facing area when applying D&I because they fail to see the business case results. Controversies such as the one created by H&M arise or products created specifically for a minority audience may not get adopted. Digging a little deeper into the endeavor, we often find that the staff was trying to fulfill a quota (mirroring) and was never formally developed on an inclusive approach to their target market, which includes understanding personal, group, and corporate-wide biases. We often find a lack of inclusion awareness and skills hampers the full and successful engagement of customers and clients. As of the writing of this book, Facebook, the largest social media site, has more than 2.2 billion monthly users. Although more than half of its user base is female, the company has only recently placed two women on its board. It is hard to fathom how a company can effectively manage a demographic externally when it fails to manage it internally.

It wasn't until 2018 that Facebook seated its first African American board member. Was this done to quell public relations concerns because it is a publicly traded company? Or did the company finally see the value of a more inclusive board?

Online Facebook stores (online retail portals on Facebook) have opened and closed quickly because of a lack of customer engagement. Although Facebook has tried to secure the recruitment business in many ways by selling recruitment advertising and integrating recruitment apps, it still falls way behind other online entities such as job boards and LinkedIn that have a fraction of its audience.

Acquire

An effective Reach has a solid business case in quick adoption and eventually client acquisition, which brings us to the next phase—Acquire.

The Acquire stage of the customer relationship is key to setting foundational expectations. The initial images your clientele receives in the Reach stage help to set their first impression. The visual impression of your team either supports or conflicts with this impression. Is your team in uniform or in business or casual attire? Are they neat or unkempt in appearance? Is the team all men or all women? Is there a real diversity in staffing? Is it an army or a team of one? Because most companies like to put their best foot forward in the initial conversations, any visual conflict can detract from a good foundation. For example, your reach advertising shows a diverse team of different ethnicities, ages, and abilities and yet the actual team is fairly homogenous, with very little differentiation in any of these areas.

The real test of inclusion is in client engagement. During a sales meeting at which a firm was selling its sales methodology development, Mason noticed that the two presenters focused the majority of their attention on an older white male in the room. Everything was running behind that day, so in the interest of time there was no formal introduction of those at the table. The presenters ended their talk by asking this gentleman what he thought. There was some small talk and then Mason and the team convened to speak privately about the services offered. The chief sales officer, whom we will call Julie, stood up and said, "Odd, I liked their book, but obviously from their presentation, it must only be about selling to one type of person." The consulting company assumed the older white gentleman was the CSO and ignored the others. However, those the presenters ignored were the decision makers, while the gentleman they'd chiefly addressed was a technician from the IT department there to answer any questions about the company's e-learning system.

Needless to say, the presenters fell into a trap of their own unconscious biases. How we are developed to create an inclusive team internally or how we are managed inclusively will affect our approach with external clients. The presenters' unchecked bias ultimately cost their firm a $1 million-per-year development deal.

Sometimes unconscious bias is conveyed not by how we are engaging the client, but by how we are engaging each other in front of the client. Is there mutual respect on the team for one another's roles and ideas? Does the client note one dominating subset of the team muffling another group? Does the team take turns in leadership roles?

It is not uncommon in larger deals or with requests for proposals (RFP) for the client to ask about your commitment to diversity and inclusion. Not having an effective existing strategy will immediately put a company in a bidding disadvantage or, in some cases, will totally disqualify it from the bid. Some quick metrics for a business case in this area are:

- What percentage of RFPs include information on internal D&I initiatives?

- Has there been a change in the demographics of decision makers?
- What are the year-over-year sales of teams who have been provided D&I leadership development versus those who have not?

Ever greater numbers of clients are holding their partners accountable beyond the acquisition stage. Some have even begun to track and score their service providers' commitment to diversity. In a March 6, 2012, *Wall Street Journal* article, William Von Hoene, Exelon's executive vice president for legal and finance, noted, "We know that diversity and inclusion is a value that must be top of mind and integrated into everything we do, and we expect our partner organizations to approach business the same way. This extends to our outside financial partners, as they provide services critical to our success." The article highlighted awards Exelon was bestowing upon its service partners for "exemplifying the corporation's commitment to diversity and inclusion." In 2017 alone, Exelon devoted $2 billion in expenditures to diversity suppliers.

Develop

It is during the Develop stage of the relationship that firms with a dedication to inclusion will shine, as exemplified by the companies that received Exelon's honors. Exelon is a $33 billion company, and when you are vying for contracts with such a company, any way you can shine is going to be valuable. Exelon's practice offers a living, breathing business case for an external D&I approach. And this company is not alone. As companies see a benefit internally for inclusion, they are finding that vendors with a commitment to diversity also benefit the business. On the innovation front, as we discussed earlier, a more innovative service partner supports the company's market leader goals.

During the Develop stage, there is a need to broaden relationships with many individuals at a client organization. Going "deep and wide" is a phrase commonly heard in sales meetings: it means finding influencers, coaches, and other buyers within the same organization. The stronger and higher quality your client relationships, the better your chance of upselling during good times or securing business when times are tough. Account executives who have not been developed to deal with diverse groups of decision makers will find it difficult to go beyond the initial decision maker. They will rely on those they feel most connected with, and may lose opportunities to expand the business.

Inspire

Worse than failing at account penetration is losing the client altogether. A phenomenon that is common in many of our personal relationships may also be common in our business relationships: there comes a time when each party has stopped being intrigued by the other. This vital time is what we refer to as the Inspire stage. The relationship is either sink or swim at this level; actually, it is more like synchronize swim, or drown. It is not good enough to be simply good enough: you need to wow your clients and exceed expectations. This is true for your product and/or service, but it is especially true for building your rapport across difference. At the Inspire stage, even the strongest bonds are tested.

eXit

Sales reps who are untrained in the nuances of inclusion and/or insider–outsider dynamics may find it quite difficult to deepen their existing relationships while developing team rapport. How often have we seen decision makers move on and the second-in-charge take the helm? If the rep has not cemented a bond with the entire team, she will be at a loss when the new leader wants to make her mark.

Three important goals the client-facing team needs to accomplish prior to a breakup talk are to:

- Develop relationships with the entire client team (not just the signer)
- Create synergy with your clients not only with regard to services, but more importantly with respect to rapport
- Provide a sense of value beyond the price and product

The internal team can only fully accomplish the above points if they have been developed to understand their own personal biases and to reach across differences. The business case is easily measured in this stage by percentage of renewal reports and growth in long-term clients. Low renewal rates and stagnant growth with long-term clients may point to an inability of the client-facing team to develop a true partnership.

If the partnership is not blossoming (more relationships, higher engagement), then it will not be surprising if the client moves to the last stage: eXit. In the eXit stage, teams may look to lay blame on the client or the service offered. As with any breakup, the sales team may have feelings of revenge and ill will toward the client. Comments such as, "That decision maker has no idea what she is doing," or "They were far more trouble than they were worth," are telltale signs that the sales team did not have a good rapport with the client.

Exiting gracefully and with understanding is important for future business. Client-facing teams experiencing a client loss need to focus on:

- Managing a successful transition.
- Maintaining relationships.
- Securing future recommendations/referrals.

True relationships will survive the customer termination. Reps need to create an inclusive, welcoming environment during this time. Although your company may no longer be servicing this particular client, it is very likely that several of the client's employees were not in favor of this separation. Maintaining relationships and keeping an open approach may pay off in future recommendations. It may also secure future business as these contacts move into decision-making positions. The business case in the eXit stage is measured in "win back" clients and referrals.

In the past, anecdotal evidence has supported the business case for corporate diversity and inclusion. As our industries have become more integrated and global, it is hard to ignore study after study that proves beyond a doubt the dividend provided by investing in an inclusive environment. It directly affects the way the company hires, retains, and engages quality talent. Innovation is higher. Productivity is higher. The way we engage our fellow employees is directly linked to the way we engage our external clients and partners. Employees will leave because of poor management. Similarly, clients will leave because of poor relationships.

A strategy for diversity and inclusion team development should look at the full spectrum of business activities, from advertising and marketing to employee engagement (i.e., talent acquisition and management) to client engagement. Solid business cases abound in each and every segment.

Takeaways

- ✓ The business case should prove a decrease in expenses and/or an increase in revenue.
- ✓ Business cases that prove increases in revenue gain greater attention and budget.
- ✓ Innovation is directly linked to a diverse, inclusive environment.
- ✓ Mirroring is a tactic, not a strategy.

✓ How we treat our colleagues internally is reflected in our relationships externally. Greater diversity of decision makers, due to changing demographics, requires higher personal awareness and better developed skills to engage and build relationships across difference. A company reluctant to change internally will find it difficult to compete in a global environment.

✓ Clients are demanding that their partners reflect their own commitment to inclusion.

Discussion Point

Mary was recently hired as the Chief Diversity Officer for a major credit card processing company. The company has more than ten thousand employees across the United States, one-third of whom are in the sales department. The industry was facing a huge influx of start-up, Internet-based processing firms with innovative solutions. Use of credit cards was up, but clients saw credit card processing as a commodity and often sought the cheapest alternative.

The CDO position was new for the company and was initiated mainly by its legal counsel. Mary was tasked by the VP of HR, her direct manager, with assessing the company's current "diversity profile." She was to determine any areas where the company fell short and create a plan of action to move the company forward.

Mary understood the need to be in compliance with legal guidelines, but believed that focusing on diversity alone, without attention to inclusion development, was a mistake. At the time, there was no budget allocated to her one-person department. Her first presentation, after one month, to the VP of HR and his team was meant to provide her assessment and suggested course of action.

Given the information above, how would you answer the following questions?

- Putting yourself in Mary's shoes, what is your first opinion of the company's view of D&I? Why?
- Do you believe there is a business case for Mary to make for inclusion development? Why?
- Who do you suggest Mary should speak with to build the business case?
- Is the VP of HR an optimal senior leader to manage Mary? Why or why not?
- Is there a business case in a commodity-based, price-driven industry for developing the staff on diversity and inclusion? Explain.

3

Understanding Key D&I Concepts

Conversations about unconscious bias and insider–outsider dynamics can easily be lost in the noise of the daily office grind. There are sales to be made, technology to be innovated and maintained, and bills to be paid. Often, development needs around inclusion can feel secondary to the personal, group, or corporate mission. Even for a leader dedicated to inclusion, putting together all of the pieces needed to fully understand how D&I impacts daily life can be daunting. A senior executive might have a leadership course at the beginning of the year and then a webinar six months later. Something about D&I goals might show up on his performance review. His manager might talk about increasing the diversity of the staff. Active employee resource groups or affinity networks can offer a multitude of opportunities for leaders to be involved and visible. It can feel like a thousand-piece puzzle, with random pieces doled out one at a time. Worse yet, there's no picture on the box cover to show where the pieces might fit.

For this very reason, The Dagoba Group borrowed an idea from the alternative energy industry. Like the diversity and inclusion arena, the alternative energy industry also had complex issues that a mass audience needed to understand before they would change their behavior. Infographics became the industry's tool of choice. Using this approach, we introduced a visual mapping tool to give leadership the picture on the puzzle box cover. Visual maps can help highlight areas where key inclusion concepts play a role. The key concepts we will discuss in this chapter are:

- Intent and impact
- Unconscious bias
- Insider–outsider dynamics
- Levels of systems

Each of these concepts plays a role in our daily work. Let's first paint a picture of a typical day for a manager we will call Kim. Kim is a composite of managers we have interacted with over the past twenty years. We believe you will find a lot of similarities between her typical day and yours.

A Typical Senior Manager's Day

Kim started her day with an hour-long commute, which was fifteen minutes shorter than normal. Along the way she had two conference calls. One was with an employee on the East Coast who was already three hours into his day and needed coaching on how to deal with the new client project management process. The second call was to screen a potential new hire for a software engineer position. Kim had been up late the night before dealing with an executive presentation. Between the calls and the lack of sleep, she wondered how she got to the parking lot so quickly. "Thank you autopilot," she said jokingly to herself.

During the hurried trek from the company's front door to her office she encountered three "quick minute" conversations and two requests for meetings. The first two hours of the day were blocked off to start and finish her staff evaluation forms; they'd originally been due the previous week, but she'd gotten a reprieve due to some last-minute travel needs. As a VP of Operations, she had seven direct reports to evaluate. Unlike some of her peers, she saw a lot of value in the evaluations and took the process seriously.

Although her office door was closed, a knock came on the door from her HR representative, asking if she was going to make it to the talk on Women in the Workplace. Kim responded, "I don't really have time for extracurricular activities today." An hour into the process, a call from the CEO required her to go to his office to discuss an operational challenge he'd recently discovered. The challenge turned out to be a software glitch that they hoped the yet-to-be-hired software engineer would be able to fix quickly.

Before Kim realized it, it was already noon and she was running on empty. Black coffee and the leftover birthday cake she'd found in the kitchen had lost their boost. She was happy the company put in a new executive cafeteria, which allowed her to grab lunch without too many distractions. Walking in, she found the usual cadre of individuals. At the table by the window sat a few people she privately referred to as the Wharton group. They were a rather rowdy group of Wharton graduates who ranged from director level to CFO. If she sat next to them she'd get no work done. Kim politely smiled to the two SVPs from the regional branch at the next table and then looked for her exit. Near the door was a much quieter crowd known as the women's lunch network, which consisted of a group of executive women from HR to Legal to Marketing. Sitting near them would no doubt precipitate an invite to join them. Instead, Kim took her lunch back to her desk. She received a few glances from a couple of the women when she passed the door.

After a few planned operational tactical meetings, Kim dove back into her evaluations right when Angela knocked on the door. The company had instituted an executive mentoring program for high-potential individuals of underrepresented groups. Angela, born and raised in South Korea, was Kim's mentee. Kim's last mentee, Raymond, had been promoted, so Angela was excited to be assigned to Kim. Kim forgot it was their monthly meeting. She'd already had to cancel the meeting twice, so she knew she could not just cancel this one. Kim sighed visibly and waved Angela in the door, letting her know that it was a very busy day and she was working on little sleep.

Kim had not prepared, so she asked Angela what she wanted to talk about. Normally, the mentor had an agenda for the meeting, so Angela was caught a little off guard, but she quickly mentioned a few topics. During the conversation, Kim had to excuse herself three times to answer the phone and "shoot off a quick email on a priority issue that just came up." Instead of an hour, the talk lasted thirty-three minutes before Kim ended the conversation so she could get back to work. She promised Angela she would be more prepared for the next meeting and thanked her for being so flexible. At that point, Raymond happened to be walking by and popped his head in to say hi to his former mentor. Kim and Raymond chatted idly for a few minutes as Angela left the room quietly.

After Raymond left, Kim wondered whether Angela had the confidence to take on a leadership role. The company really needed outgoing individuals like Raymond for its senior management positions. A quick look at the clock told her she would never get the evaluations done on time, so she did what most of her peers did and quickly checked off the assessment forms to get them completed. She did not have time to write out comments, so everyone basically got good scores. This way there would be no personnel issues she would have to deal with down the road.

On her commute home, Kim had two more phone interviews with software engineers. The last one was a referral by Raymond. Given the new attention by the CEO, she thought it was a safe bet to extend an offer to Raymond's referral. Because the engineer will be working a lot with Raymond's department she wanted the person to be a good fit. The battery on her phone was just about dead when she pulled into the driveway.

Intent and Impact

Kim's day is likely not too different from most managers at any company. Her level of commitment is often found in senior leadership ranks. One can easily see, from the account of Kim's day, that she has the best intention of doing what is right for the company and devotes a considerable chunk of her life to her job. If she has good intent when it comes to managing people and believes in a meritocracy, how would diversity and inclusion development help her or, for that matter, help the company move forward?

The answer to the above question may be in the resulting impact. Intent frequently does not equal impact. As you have and will continue to read in this book, it is rare that we encounter a leader with anything but good intent. In order to move the company forward, though, leaders' intentions have to create the desired impact. For example, you may intend to put out a grease fire in the kitchen. You rush to the sink, fill a pot of water, and throw it on the fire. Your very good intention is to douse the fire. Your experience and knowledge up to that point was that water puts out fire. However, if you have taken a fire safety course, you know that water on a grease fire only causes the grease to explode, possibly injuring those nearby and spreading the fire. The fire crisis is now amplified by a factor of ten.

Have you witnessed a relatively minor situation at work get magnified in the wrong way when the manager did not have the appropriate skills to deal with the issue? You are most likely shaking your head in affirmation right now. We have all seen or been in those situations ourselves. A mismanaged event may not lead to a bigger crisis but rather to an unintended impact. Take, for example, a company that believes allowing the creation of employee resource groups (ERGs) goes against its "meritocracy" principles because ERGs inherently exclude other groups of individuals. Though the intent is to honor individuality and meritocracy, the company may inadvertently be creating two unintended impacts. It may be sending a message that it does not value differences and could be missing an opportunity to leverage diversity. ERGs have been debated in many corporations. Corporations that fully leverage the "resource" piece of the ERG have tremendous returns in terms of employee engagement, innovation, and customer engagement. Officially recognizing or not recognizing ERGs is always a decision made with a best-for-the-company intent. Managing the impact of this decision is where leadership skill is required.

Looking back at Kim's day, where do you see the impact of her actions not matching her good intent? Let's focus a little on Kim's behavior and on common systemic corporate exclusion practices. During the recent bailout of the big three auto companies, those of us not in the industry discovered how isolated executives were from their staffs. They had private elevators, bathrooms, and cafeterias. These facilities were likely created with the best of intents; they allowed executives quick, easy, and uninterrupted movement in and out of their offices. Executives had a place to entertain high-profile guests and reward employees.

When brought into the public light, however, the special facilities had an impact vastly different from the intention. The separation was seen as pure elitism. The executive management teams were seen by the public as out of touch with reality. Kim's use of the executive cafeteria removes her from the general employee population. Her intent is to get more work done, but the impact may be that she is scarcer to her staff, creating demands on her time like those made on the walk into the office or by frequent drop-ins.

There are many areas in Kim's day where we can see the intent–impact mismatch. We will focus on another that is very common within corporations. Providing critical feedback during the evaluation process can be stressful for both those managing and those being managed. It is no wonder many managers simply give a good score so everyone is happy. Kim had the intent to keep organizational peace. The resulting impact will be a staff that does not have the critically important conversations they need in order to grow and, in parallel, to grow the company. The cost also comes, as it often does, when an employee needs to be let go for performance and shows up with his lawyer and his stellar evaluations in hand.

This dynamic is exacerbated by diversity. Leaders often find it more difficult to give feedback to people who are different from themselves. This can be due simply to a lack of knowledge about what the other person needs and responds to. This dynamic shows up most powerfully not in annual performance evaluations, but in the day-to-day opportunities where "just in time" feedback can have the biggest impact. Generally, the less affinity, comfort, and common ground two people have together, the more difficult it is to develop an easy rapport. When there is a lack of knowledge or rapport, it is harder for the manager to know how to give direct, clear, and helpful feedback. And if there is perceived pressure to "walk on eggshells" with underrepresented groups, there is even less of a likelihood that helpful feedback will be delivered. This is a lose–lose–lose scenario. The employee not getting the feedback loses the opportunity to improve, the manager loses some level of full engagement from an employee, and, ultimately, the organization loses productivity.

There is also a fourth loss possible here. A lack of clear feedback can create weaker performance among underrepresented groups, and this can create a self-fulfilling prophecy that is rarely shouted but often whispered—that these underrepresented groups (women, people of color, minority ethnic groups, gays and lesbians, etc.) just aren't competent.

Companies don't make their performance ratings public, but we can look at evaluations in public organizations like school systems. In 2011, the Guilford County School systems in North Carolina had an amazing crop of teachers, according to their performance ratings. Of the nearly three thousand teachers, less than .3 percent were given ratings of "not demonstrated," which is roughly equivalent to "below average" or "does not meet expectations" in the corporate world. Now, there could be a hundred reasons why the ratings were heavily weighted on the positive side. One of the reasons was almost assuredly the same as Kim's intent. Unfortunately for Guilford County, the school system may now have sub-par teachers who believe they are performing to expectations and do nothing to improve their work.

When managing a diverse group of individuals, a leader needs to be cognizant of the resulting impact of her behavior and words. There are many managers who believe they only need to have good intent, and that D&I development is for those who are "prejudiced" or who "discriminate." Ask BP's chairman of the board, Carl-Henric Svanberg, about his intent when he called those impacted by the Gulf oil spill "the small people." There is no doubt he had the best of intentions during the press conference, but the impact of his words had a considerable negative effect on the company's already damaged public image. Hopefully, you will agree that good intent is not enough; leaders need to develop their skills to manage for the best impact.

Matching intent with impact is a general leadership challenge. However, as we have intimated above and will discuss more directly now, failures of intent can be exacerbated when diversity is present. This is simply because 1) we just don't know enough about those who are different from us; 2) our unconscious biases blur our vision; and 3) insider–outsider dynamics predict an intent–impact mismatch.

Unconscious Bias

Why is it that good intent so often fails to yield a good impact? One explanation that is gaining popularity is the concept of unconscious bias. Bias has a negative connotation for most of us, so we tend to believe we are not biased. We tell ourselves we truly believe everyone is equal and everyone deserves a fair chance. We take everything on its merit except when we don't. Let's start small. If you were ever part of the process of naming a child, you will come directly into contact with bias. Everyone has experience with one name or another that is connected to something negative. The Sarah you knew in grade school was mean. Penelope sounded like the old lady next door who left her dentures out most of the time. Madison is the name of a high school girlfriend who left you at the prom. All of these experiences, good and bad, have biased us on names.

Okay, you are thinking that just concerns names and has no impact on work. The examples above concern very conscious choices. You know you are biased in these cases. Now let's speed up the processing of names, to approximate the activity of reviewing résumés. A Ladders-sponsored study tracked a group of recruiters for thirty days. The recruiters wore special eye-tracking devices that detected where and for how long they looked at parts of a résumé. Prior to the experiment, the researchers asked recruiters how much time they spend reviewing each résumé. The overwhelming answer was four to five minutes. If you are familiar with the talent acquisition process, a bell might go off in your head at that answer, telling you this is nearly impossible given the volume of résumés typically received for each job posting. The study showed that recruiters spent an average of six seconds reviewing each résumé. A candidate's résumé was categorized into the rejection or further review pile within six seconds.

The first thing recruiters looked at was the candidate's name, which meant that everything they looked at afterward was filtered through their thoughts about the person's name. As you read in chapter 2, an MIT study demonstrated that a simple name change either increased or decreased a person's chances of an interview by 50 percent. Now, are these recruiters consciously discriminating? We will go on the record saying we believe they all had the best intent to find the best talent. The challenge lies in our unconscious biases.

The first step to mitigating unintended bias on our decisions is becoming aware of our individual biases. Actually, the true first step is to accept that we have them. We all have biases. You would not be human without them. They range from the route we take home to the people we feel an affinity with to how we decide on the evaluation for our team members. Where do you see unconscious bias perhaps taking a role in Kim's day? Think of all the little and sometimes subtle behaviors that result from unconscious, unintentional bias. These behaviors often involve tones of voice, methods of engagement, or vernacular that changes, typically along dimensions of difference. For a quick and easy example, think about the way you speak to your child compared with the way you speak to your significant other. Has your partner ever accused you of speaking to him or her "like a child"? Have you made this statement? The difference can be simply tone or choice of words. Although they are small, these micro-inequities can build up over time to create major management obstacles.

Let's look at Kim's choice of words when she told the HR representative she could not attend the "Women in the Workplace" workshop. She called it an "extracurricular activity." She was in a rush and probably thought it was a worthwhile event, but her choice of words could be considered demeaning. Are there areas where Kim's actions or words may show a preference for men in the workplace? Her attention and time for her former mentee Raymond was more welcoming when compared with her unpreparedness and lack of time for current mentee Angela. Does Angela's Asian background lead Kim to perceive Angela's quiet demeanor as unsuitable for leadership? What about Kim's avoidance of lunch with her female colleagues? Any isolated action is small and can be excused. After all, her intent is to get her work done. Isn't that what she was hired to do? When the actions are added up, however, they could create the perception that Kim is not treating both genders equally. Because she's an executive, these "little behaviors" manifesting from unconscious, unintentional bias carry more weight, as the working populace often looks toward executives to set the tone.

How could Kim have tweaked her actions to create a less ambiguous perception? First, Kim would need to become more aware of her behavior and its impact on the team. This is not easy to accomplish, but with the right development Kim could be perceived more positively. When faced with the "Women in the Workplace" workshop she could not attend, Kim could have said, "Wow, I would love to attend this very important workshop, but I am really overwhelmed with deadlines today. Could you send me a meeting invite for the next event, and please let everyone know I apologize for not attending today?"

After her session with Angela, when Raymond stopped by, Kim could have said, "Raymond, I would really love to chat, but I just had to cut short my time with Angela. If you have some time, could you spend thirty minutes with her talking about how you were able to leverage the mentorship program?" Or when Kim was passing by the lunch table of female colleagues, she could have said, "Wish I could join you, but I am knee deep in evaluations. If you would have me, I would love to lunch next week when the calendar lets up. Oh, and if any of you knows of a great software engineer, please let me know."

Can you imagine how these alternate responses would have had a better cumulative impact than Kim's original actions? Simple tweaks to small messages can make a huge difference. Micro inequities are often felt most keenly by what we call the outsider, or subordinated, group.

Does Kim's opinion about what will make a successful leader in the organization reflect bias? Does being around aggressive male executives have any impact on her evaluation of Angela? Could the culture be self-fulfilling? Do company executives systemically see aggressive men as high-potential leaders because all of the existing leaders are aggressive men? Does the corporation have an affinity bias for Wharton graduates? Are these graduates more successful than those from other universities or even individuals who don't have college or graduate degrees? Would you have hired Steve Jobs, Bill Gates, Peter Jennings, or Mark Zuckerberg? None of them graduated from college. If Warren Buffet had gone to a business school other than Wharton, would he be any less an investment guru? Would you still have hired him if he'd graduated from the University of Virginia?

Does Kim's bias toward Raymond make his referral any more of a fit for the software engineering job? Or does it continue to feed the engine of likeness? Unconscious bias is not intentional and is not only individual. It can be embedded in a team setting and in organizational processes. Biases toward a particular group of colleges or employers can be instituted in recruitment practices, leading to a lack of flexibility in evaluating other qualified candidates. It is not enough to have good intentions.

Insider–Outsider Dynamics

Every team or organization has insider and outsider groups. These groups could be based on things such as age, ethnicity, gender, sexual orientation, or on education level, class, or geography. The insider group is the group with more power, while the outsider group is subordinated in terms of power. This is about groups, not about individuals. Many individuals in outsider groups, for example, do not behave in a subordinated manner. The reference point is of a systemic nature, and insider–outsider dynamics pervade most organizations and teams. Even within close teams, insider–outsider dynamics are present. Gender dynamics, for example, can easily show up in teams. People not of the dominant culture may find it harder to develop affinity with their colleagues and claim a full voice on the team. To take a less theoretical view of this dynamic, let's examine Kim's day once again.

There are a few glaring insider groups that appear in Kim's day. The hierarchies at firms automatically create in-groups and out-groups, with executives constituting an in-group. The in-group has certain privileges, such as the executive cafeteria at Kim's company. Within this insider group, we can easily view the dynamics that group individuals together at lunch tables. Being a graduate of Wharton in this firm puts you in an insider group. Gender is a separating factor, with men occupying the insider group. Field executives would likely describe themselves as being in the outsider group compared with corporate executives. Very often we see departmental insider groups, depending on the corporate culture and type of industry. Sales may be a powerful insider group at companies like PwC or Prudential, while IT may be the group with power at companies like Google or Facebook.

Have you heard that being in a particular department or working for a certain boss would "put you on the fast track to promotion"? Being affiliated with the in-group can often provide an unspoken advantage when it comes to hiring or promotion. It is not uncommon for one to be an outsider within an in-group. It is clear from the day's depiction that being a woman in Kim's organization puts her in an outsider group even though as an executive she is a member of an insider group. Outsider groups must work much harder to stay level with the insider groups. For example, a 2014 Columbia University study suggested that women applying for STEM positions had to be 15 percent better than men in order to be equally considered. How much harder does Angela have to work just to stay even with Raymond, in terms of visibility and career development opportunities? There is an inherent unfair advantage for insider groups and disadvantage for outsider groups at many levels.

Level of Systems Framework

To understand and shift insider–outsider group dynamics and to minimize the impact of unconscious bias, there needs to be a systemic view. We offer the Level of Systems Framework as a way to understand the broader process of creating sustainable inclusion. There are four distinct levels: individual, group/team, organization, and marketplace. Keep in mind that although the levels are distinct, they do bleed into one another; we will go into this a little later, but first let's define each level.

The Individual Level

The individual level may seem quite self-explanatory. It is the person: it is you, me, the boss, or your staff member. At the individual level we are all unique, though there may be similarities across ethnicities, cultures, gender, and so on. Individual histories and experiences influenced by these aspects of difference create very different people. Mason is one of six brothers and two sisters, all of whom grew up in the same Irish Catholic household with the same parents and culture. However, the children span the political spectrum from Libertarian to Republican to Democrat. They all attended different universities and went into very different careers. Their tastes in music, movies, and friends are about as different as they can get. However, growing up they encountered different people (school friends, groups, and one another), which helped to create a different personality imprint for each. Their backgrounds look the same from a distance, but up close they are all different. In fact, is any human being exactly like another?

The Group and Team Level

At the individual level our accumulated experiences make us unique, but we are heavily influenced by our shared groups. Being from a particular socioeconomic background will expose one to certain influences and opportunities. Affluent families may travel more extensively or send their children on foreign exchanges, to summer camps, or perhaps to private schools. Growing up in a different country or being an outsider in your own country also shapes the individual. Within the United States, we see geographic influences when comparing the Northeast with the South (or what is often referred to as the Bible Belt) or with the West Coast. Being a woman in a country where no woman has ever held the highest political office and where women have historically been paid less for the same work impacts the individual. Being disabled in a world made for the able-bodied is yet another example. Racial history and current bias mean that white people and people of color have both different experiences and different perceptions of their experiences on a day-to-day basis. In many neighborhoods across the United States, walking or driving down the streets can be a very different experience for a white person versus a person of color. DWB, "driving while black," is a term that refers to a type of racial profiling in which a person of color is more likely to be pulled over by police simply because of the color of their skin. Our group memberships frequently have more impact on our perspectives, experiences, and behavior than does our individuality. We will talk more about our group memberships in chapter 7, "Dimensions of Difference."

Our group memberships are not neutral. As we have discussed, there are insider–outsider dynamics that are inherent with group membership. These dynamics show up as patterns in the organization, in terms of developmental assignments, performance ratings, and promotion to name a few. They also show up, sometimes powerfully, as dynamics on teams and can profoundly impact performance. Teams are more and more frequently the primary structure in which work gets done. How individuals, vis a vis their group identities, are able to flourish on teams will have an important impact on the organization. Insider–outsider dynamics, if not addressed, will severely interfere with the goal of creating an inclusive organization and negatively impact the opportunity for innovation. An organization that wants sustainable inclusion will need to address the unproductive impact of these insider–outsider dynamics.

The Organizational Level

All of these teams and processes are embedded at the organizational level. For one reason or another, a company has determined to recruit from targeted schools, base promotions on certain kinds of characteristics, and design a culture to reflect certain attributes. We spoke earlier about how groups are distinct but have blurred boundaries. At the organizational level this is often the case. Those who decide which schools to target are basing their decision upon their own preference or perceptions. In Kim's company, there may be a preference for Wharton. Perhaps the company's founder was a Wharton graduate who brought in some of his classmates, which perpetuated a culture in which the definition of an executive included a Wharton degree.

If we move from talent acquisition to talent management, we can look at the talent review and promotion process. We can ask what biases might be embedded in that process, which competencies really matter, whether there are controls for unconscious bias, and who makes the final decisions. Our individual biases about our group memberships get embedded systemically, and then feedback to all of the groups and individuals in the company creates a self-fulfilling organizational culture, reflecting and reinforcing the biases and preferences of the most powerful people in the company.

The Marketplace Level

Ultimately, any organization needs to pay attention to one additional level of system—the marketplace. The company's success in seeing, understanding, and engaging its current and future customer base is critical to its success as an enterprise. A company's brand will have a D&I component, whether the company is aware of it or not. In a future that looks more diverse, not less, the marketplace level of system is even more critical.

Applying Key Concepts to Create Inclusion

Kim struggled with bandwidth all day when trying to complete her employee evaluations. If the company believed evaluations were important for building a stronger team, could it have instituted some systemic changes that would emphasize this priority? Here are a few ideas:

- Corporate blackouts: The company could set aside set times when no meetings would be scheduled, in order to free up time for evaluations. For example, Friday mornings between eight o'clock and noon for a whole month.
- Evaluation meetings: Time could be scheduled for leaders to attend a meeting to fill out evaluations. These meetings would include a person on hand to answer any system or advisory questions.
- Incentive: A portion of the manager's bonus could be based upon her timely and thorough completion of staff evaluations. This would have a bottom-up effect when applied to all leadership.

- Rotating review: An ad hoc project team made up of different team members each year could review employee assessments/grading. This process would help ensure a less biased approach and keep everyone actively engaged in the process. Determine whether there are trends associated with dimensions of difference such as gender.

According to a study by Stanford University's Clayman Institute, managers perceive women as having better team-based skills, while they see men as being more independent. In the same study, evaluations of women included twice as many references to team accomplishments, rather than individual achievements, as those of men. These evaluation biases may steer more women toward support roles and men toward leadership roles. Making the evaluation process better helps all staff and particularly helps outsider groups, because these groups are more likely to get short shrift in these processes. Lack of systemic processes that make employee assessment a priority often results in a higher degree of unconscious bias and ultimately leads to less effective development of all staff, and particularly outsider groups. In the end, Kim chose the path of least resistance, which is what most managers do when under pressure. While typical and understandable, this behavior only increases the impact of unconscious bias and insider–outsider dynamics. This is true not only of the performance evaluation process: to create an inclusive culture, all of the talent acquisition and talent management processes must be reviewed and changed to remove unintended bias.

Many of us can relate and even sympathize with Kim. She has good intentions to do what is best for her team and company. Without the proper development, Kim has to rely on her instincts and react to the culture, which has entrenched power groups and influence at each level of system. Her unintended subtle messages, when perceived by others, may have an unintended impact. Slowly, her team, her company, and even she may miss the dividend that comes with a culture of inclusion.

Takeaways

- ✓ Inclusion should be part of our daily decisions.
- ✓ A sustainable inclusion effort must include change at four distinct levels: individual, group/team, organization, and marketplace.
- ✓ One level of system influences and reinforces the others.
- ✓ Good intent is not good enough when the impact does not match.
- ✓ Subtle messages or little behaviors accumulate to have a large impact.
- ✓ Having biases is human. Managing the impact of our biases is leadership.
- ✓ Small changes in our processes can dramatically shift results.
- ✓ Every team has insider and outsider groups.
- ✓ Most are not born with an innate sense for how to manage inclusively. It is a skill set that requires continual development, much like any other leadership skill set.

Discussion Point

Reviewing Kim's day, discuss the following questions:

- ◆ Of which insider and outsider groups do you think Kim is a member? How about Raymond and Angela?
- ◆ What do you think the long-term impact of Kim's management style will be?
- ◆ Which level of system is Kim most influenced by?
- ◆ In what way does unconscious bias impact Kim's talent acquisition decisions?

4

Framing a Sustainable Inclusion Initiative

We interviewed dozens of chief diversity officers, asking them the same question, and received a very common response across industries, backgrounds, and experiences. The question went something like this: "It is often said that the role of the CDO is to work him/herself out of a job. Have you heard this statement before and what is your response?" The first response from the CDO is typically a chuckle. Every one of them has heard this statement and some have, at one point in their careers, said it themselves. They then speak in metaphors about other chief officer positions: Once the books are set, does the chief financial officer no longer have a job? When an IT project is complete, is there no reason to have a chief technology officer?

Is there an ultimate end point for diversity and inclusion? Or a critical mass? If we just trained enough people, changed their attitudes, and got them to value difference, would that be enough? Can we drive inclusion by doing enough "diversity events?" The answer to all of these questions is "no." A large-scale strategic change initiative requires a sustained effort and active change management. Many organizations know this lesson well from other change initiatives. Just as there are always more challenges for a chief technology officer, a chief diversity officer is continually tasked with moving the company toward ever-higher levels of inclusion or at the very least not allowing it to regress.

Leaders need a broad view of what it takes to create real and sustainable inclusion in an organization. In the pages ahead, we will build on the level of systems model to discuss how power moves from the individual to the marketplace level. This framework will help you think strategically about how to construct your D&I strategy. Along the way we will share some typical pitfalls. D&I is continuously evolving as the organization grows, and there is no finish line.

Corporate Safety Programs as a Model for Creating Sustainable Change

An apt comparison to D&I initiatives are organizational change programs designed to increase safety in the workplace. Safety efforts, undertaken by many large companies, are large-scale organizational change efforts. Creating day-to-day safety in the workplace requires a broad range of efforts at multiple levels within the organization. Individuals need information and awareness at a basic level to change their attitudes and behavior. The organization has to look beyond individual behavior, though, and search for patterns. Are there certain safety challenges that continue to arise? Are there particular parts of the organization where there are more safety challenges than others, regardless of the level of skill or competence of the staff? Do certain jobs seem to create more safety violations than others? When those patterns are understood, broader strategies can be developed.

At another level, the culture needs to change, or evolve, in some ways. "Culture change" sounds a bit amorphous. Culture change is a term often bandied about when discussing some sort of organizational change program. In other words, an organization knows it needs to change in some way, and describes it as changing the culture. Edgar Schein, the person often credited with creating the term "corporate culture," described culture change as a substantial process that involved changing underlying assumptions. All change programs do not require a complete culture change. Culture change is often folded into so many different change initiatives such as technology, quality, or safety. Most individuals and systems alike find culture change to be extremely challenging. Inclusion doesn't usually require a full-on culture change process, however, some shifting and tweaking of the culture is usually required.

Culture is about formal and informal rules. It is about what is written down, but more importantly it is about what is not written down. For example, a culture that makes it difficult to challenge authority can inadvertently result in safety problems, regardless of established protocols: at Korean Air, significant and serious safety problems resulted from a culture in which copilots deferred to the authority of captains, even in life-or-death situations. Seven hundred lives were lost between 1970 and 1999, during which time Korean Air wrote off sixteen aircraft in serious accidents, giving it one of the worst safety records at the time. Hierarchical order was deeply embedded in Korean culture and mirrored in the cockpit, however, Boeing and Airbus were creating modern aircraft that required two equals to operate. Although the Korean Air crew was thoroughly trained in operating the aircraft (i.e., the written norms), there was no effort to parallel this technical change with a matching culture shift (i.e., the unwritten norms).

In order to overcome the strong cultural norm of being deferential to authority, Korean Air couldn't simply train pilots to fly the aircraft. It had to develop processes that allowed copilots to be assertive when it comes to safety. The programs had to impact the cultural norms. Korean Air's experience shows how creating sustainable change requires efforts at multiple levels. A change effort must impact individuals' knowledge, shift patterns that are inconsistent with the strategic direction, and impact the culture—both the written and unwritten norms

What is true for safety initiatives and other large-scale organizational change efforts is also true for diversity and inclusion initiatives, which attempt to shift historical and long-held views, attitudes, policies, and practices. Real and sustainable inclusion requires, among other things:

- A clear organizational rationale and strategy.
- A concrete connection to the company's business.
- Reward systems that incent new behaviors.
- Developed leaders and staff who can "live" the change on a day-to-day basis.

Sustainable change requires leverage in each of those areas.

Individual	Group/Team	Organization	Marketplace
• Uniqueness • Personality • Individuality	• Patterns of experience • "In" / "Out" groups	• Behavioral norms • Policies and practices • Systems and process • Images of leadership	• Image • Client engagement • Business growth through relationship building

FIGURE 4-1 Levels of Systems Framework

The Framework for Sustainable Inclusion Model, influenced by the Dimensions of Diversity model by Dr. Kate Kirkham and Elsie Y. Cross and Associates, and the Level of Systems model from the Gestalt Institute of Cleveland, describes the four most critical levels in an organization when it comes to creating sustainable inclusion. "Sustainable" is an important word here. It is meant to convey change that is both lasting and resilient, something that goes beyond the "flavor of the month." Power is at the core of this model. Power increases with movement to a higher and broader level of system. The most powerful (and thus sustainable) change is one in which all four levels are being leveraged in an aligned, consistent way.

The Individual, Interpersonal Level of Change

Too often, D&I work is viewed as primarily about shifting attitudes. It is seen as an individual, interpersonal challenge (i.e., to what extent one is able to treat fairly and equitably those who are different from oneself). The assumption is that changing individual attitudes and behaviors will be sufficient to create inclusion. This assumption takes many organizations down the road of training and development as the primary or sole D&I strategy. Quite often, individuals emerge from this training with important knowledge but with no way to apply that knowledge and create a lasting impact on the organization.

It is en vogue to offer some sort of "diversity training." Most organizations have jumped on this bandwagon. A 2010 SHRM poll showed that 71 percent of its member organizations offered diversity training, up from 67 percent in the 2005 survey. Training for training's sake, without a strategic plan by field experts, could create greater damage than no effort at all. It can create unfulfilled expectations and cause confusion within the organization when employees do not know how to integrate it into their overall business goals. This can end up supporting the notion that diversity and inclusion are about "the right thing to do" but not substantively related to the business. A *Time Magazine* article noted a study that found decades of diversity training had no measurable impact in obtaining diversity goals related to hiring, promotions and representation in senior management. There are a number of potential reasons for this finding, but the most important reason is that training doesn't work unless it is connected to a broader change initiative that goes beyond the individual level. Think about a safety initiative that was mostly training based. People might "get it" in the classroom but not know how or be compelled to implement their learning, and thus measured levels of safety would be unlikely to change. Training for training's sake is sometimes initiated because of recent litigation or liability. This type of training is often referred to as "check the box" training, and it is most associated with HR or legal compliance. In other instances, a person unskilled in organizational development provides training without a well-planned sustainment strategy. Neither of these options would lead to a significant impact on the company's diversity and inclusion goals.

Training alone has limited impact, though it is necessary and essential as part of an inclusion change effort. How can an employee support a change effort that she doesn't understand? How can she change her behavior if she doesn't know what she is expected to do? As individuals, our own awareness and skill level are important; it is inaccurate to suggest otherwise. There are limits to creating organizational change at the individual level.

There are four major limits to focusing primarily on the individual and interpersonal levels:

1. New awareness and behavior are not supported by others. Most of us can recall receiving great insights in training programs; feeling very clear, energized, and committed at the end of a fantastic workshop; and then struggling to help others understand our insights and desired new behaviors. Often, when we "try out" our new perspective, our colleagues don't understand what we are doing or view it is a passing fad. In the worst case, we are ridiculed for new behavior. We may feel like we have insight and a fresh view of things, and may be eager to try new behaviors and take some risks. In the larger system, there can be little to no openness to our perspective, however. Thus, we have no tangible way to apply our insights productively. New insights are fragile, and when they are not supported they can disappear quickly.

Mark vividly recalls leaving a diversity workshop some thirty years ago with great insights about gender. He felt like he really understood how men and women had fundamentally different experiences in the organization, and he was eager to act and create more equitable and fair treatment. In one of his first group meetings he noticed that a woman was having a hard time getting her viewpoint heard. He was excited that he was seeing this dynamic, as it was exactly what had been discussed in the workshop! When he named what he was seeing and tried to redirect the conversation to her ideas, he mostly got blank stares, and she looked a little embarrassed. Certainly, he was not elegant in his attempt, but there was little or no support to change the gender-based norm that had already been established. He remembers feeling embarrassed and defeated. *Any change to the status quo, whether it's a way of behaving or an accepted point of view, will be difficult to sustain if it is not supported consistently and over time.*

2. A trainee's direct supervisor doesn't understand or support the intent of the training program. The death knell to any new learning comes when a participant returns from a training experience and attempts to apply that learning, only to have her manager not understand, support, or even openly reject the attempt. In an environment where it is already difficult to have open and frank conversations about diversity, a lack of support by one's manager will ensure quick reversion to the status quo. If I want to speak to my boss about my perspective as a member of a minority/outsider group and the boss is a member of the insider/majority group, the conversation could be a risky venture. Most of us have a strong set of organizational survival skills, and the first rule is usually to keep the boss happy. Our managers are our most direct connection to the organization's reward systems, and most of us want to be rewarded for the work we do. *If individuals aren't given support and rewards for new behavior, they will not sustain those new behaviors.*

3. Organizational reward systems do not support new behaviors. The best organizations explicitly reward behaviors that create success and profitability. Quite often, the rewarded behaviors are at odds with new learned behaviors from training programs. For example, changing the dynamics of a team to make it more inclusive of all team members may create some challenges in the short term that could temporarily lower productivity. Spending more time as a leader on building relationships with a more diverse cross section of employees takes time and may temporarily reduce productivity. Providing an opportunity for a stretch assignment to a staff member who has been overlooked will cost time and probably productivity in the short term. Systems that automatically penalize these short-term bumps will make it more difficult to focus on the long-term impact. To create inclusion that is sustainable, leaders have to be supported/rewarded in tangible ways for taking these steps. *Change will be temporary, even among motivated and inspired individuals, if they are not rewarded for changing their behavior and leadership.*

4. Talent-related processes do not support change. An organization's talent-related processes are where the rubber meets the road when it comes to D&I. These processes include selection and hiring, onboarding, performance feedback, career development, mentoring, and promotions. Often, the processes are designed with the intent to create objectivity, inclusion, and meritocracy but they have unintentional biases built in. For example, hiring decisions may be made by a nondiverse group that unintentionally favors those similar to them. There may even be a built-in bias to recruit from a certain employer (and thus a certain profile) due to an executive's affinity for that employer. There may be assumptions about job requirements that are unnecessary to successful performance, but which have been embedded in the job description for a long time.

A "stretch assignment" may be given to someone who has developed a strong rapport with her manager. This rapport may have resulted from affinity based on similarity. All of these factors, and many more, favor some groups over others. Enlightened and well-trained individuals may either not see these systemic dynamics or be unable to change them. These inequities and systemic biases are frequently difficult to see. Thus, even when staff is trained, the organization keeps getting the same output from the talent-related processes. ***Insights from a training program cannot overcome unintentional bias that is built into organizational systems and processes.***

Thus, change at the individual, interpersonal level is necessary but not sufficient. To fully engage a diverse workforce and create inclusion and meritocracy requires a more systemic change approach, as much of what matters to organizations goes well beyond interpersonal interactions. Still, there is important work to do at the individual level. At the individual level, awareness and skills are increased, and this is the foundation for important change efforts at other levels.

The Group and Team Level of Change

Beyond the individual level is the group level. This level is about the patterns of experience and treatment in the organization based on group membership or identity. In other words, the experiences that have more to do with group identity than with individuality. This seems paradoxical in some cultures, certainly in many Western cultures, which tend to focus on the su-premacy and value of the individual. Many of us were raised to explicitly not notice difference. Think about the explicit messages you may have received that you should be "color-blind" and not notice difference.

Some colleagues of ours tell a story about one of their children no-ticing, for perhaps the first time, someone in a wheelchair. The child's reaction was excitement, interest, and curiosity, loudly expressed! Most parents in that scenario would feel uncomfortable and try to quiet their child. Imagine yourself, if you are a white person, reacting to your child pointing out the skin color of a black person and wanting to touch it to see if it rubs off. The message that we should politely ignore differ-ence and only see people as individuals is quite strong in many Western cultures. In the United States, in particular, the notion of individuality is strong. We express a strong belief in individual rights and in the unlimited power of an individual. Seeing people as members of groups is counter-cultural at some level.

It is however, a myth that we can ignore group memberships, partic-ularly those that are visible, such as gender, age, race, some disabilities, etc. At a physiological level, we perceive these differences, consciously or not, in less than a second. At a more practical, conscious level, we simply notice difference whether we think we should or not. Our noticing of dif-ferences, as we will discuss in a later chapter on unconscious bias, affects perceptions and often behavior.

Thus, the challenge is to do both: to see people as individuals while also being aware of their group identities. Why is this important? It is important because sometimes the experiences of individuals are more based on their group membership or identity than on their individuality. This is revealed in patterns. For example, if there is a pattern of women not being seen as lead-ers or authority figures, this likely has less to do with their individual behavior and more with how they are perceived (often unconsciously) by others. If there is a pattern of Asian Americans rising to the highest nonmanagerial jobs but rarely getting promoted into leadership positions, this is probably, again, about their group identity as Asian.

Patterns can be uncovered by a close review of HR/talent management processes data or by doing interviews with a diverse cross section of staff. Think about your own experiences while we offer one of ours. We have attended literally thousands of restaurant meals in male–female groups and have seen a pattern when the check arrives. In well more than half of those meals, the check is brought to one of the men, even if the men are younger than the women at the table. These are business meetings, and the waiters often know that. This plays out in business settings as well, when the man on a team is perceived to be the leader.

There are many patterns present in organizations connected to group identity. They are present in day-to-day interactions, but also in the talent acquisition and management systems of most organizations. In one client organization, management audited the performance reviews and found the language in the reviews of men was different than that used in the reviews of women. The language in the men's reviews was more about core job skills, whereas the language in the reviews of women was more about interpersonal skills and fit. It is not uncommon to find patterns of bias in recruiting and hiring processes. Often, for example, hires are similar to the hiring manager. Sometimes job descriptions have criteria that are no longer critical to successful performance. These criteria often lead to similar people being hired, and thus they contribute to a pattern. One practice that can help forestall that pattern is to add an expiration date to all job postings; criteria can then be revised on a periodic basis so they more closely match the job's needs and to mitigate any biases unintentionally embedded in the posting.

Why do these patterns exist? In a later chapter, chapter 6, we will focus more on insider–outsider dynamics. For now, we will simply point out that these dynamics are about the power relationships between groups, about which groups tend to be favored in any given society, culture, or organization. Any aspect of difference (or group identity) likely has insider–outsider dynamics attached to it. Suffice it to say, the patterns related to group membership track closely to insider–outsider dynamics, and in fact are often the result of these dynamics.

When we describe the "group level," we are talking about group membership and identity, in other words the social identity groups to which we belong or with which we are identified. We are not talking about work groups or teams. However, many of the most important group level patterns and insider–outsider dynamics play out on work teams. The team is the primary unit where work gets done in most organizations. As the corporate population grows to hundreds and then to thousands, structures are created to effectively manage the work teams by combining them into functional or geographical groups of teams. The Center for the Study of Work Teams (CSWT) reported something we all experience in our work lives, roughly 80 percent of Fortune 500 firms will have half their employees working in teams. In recent years these teams are increasingly diverse and global, often virtual teams remotely connecting.

Although there are individual inputs, all of these inputs are coordinated through our formal team memberships. These teams need to know how to create engagement and inclusivity. Teams and team leaders need to create working norms that ameliorate the negative impact of group membership and insider–outsider dynamics, not set norms that benefit some and disadvantage others. If the loudest, deepest, and first voice into the discussion is always the one that gets followed, then meritocracy and performance will be diminished. Perhaps the most important hallmark of a successful team is its effectiveness in creating inclusivity. The fundamental proposition of the growth of teams in organizations is that a team working together will experience synergy and produce a better result than a collection of individuals working alone. This is the best-case scenario, though, and there is no guarantee.

Inclusion is the key human dynamics factor that will determine whether synergy is realized. It is challenging enough to create synergy on a team of individuals who are very similar to one another. It is even more challenging when the team is diverse. Virtually every corporation with more than $100 million in revenue has employees, vendors, clients, or all of the above in multiple countries. As we discussed in chapter 1, civil law in many countries has forced open the corporate doors to a much more diverse population. Given the huge increase in diversity in organizations in many parts of the world over the last twenty to thirty years, the ability of teams to minimize insider–outsider dynamics and maximize inclusion is of the utmost importance. When tasks require judgment and creativity, demographically diverse teams have the potential to perform better, especially under circumstances that tend to create inclusivity.

We hope that it is becoming apparent why a focus at the group level is important for creating an inclusive organization. The insider–outsider patterns we are referring to are disturbing in that they create inequities. We expect that most people are disturbed by inequity and unfairness. However, these patterns have profound business implications as well. They often result in lower levels of engagement and productivity, higher turnover, and decreased market share. The 2017 Tech Levers Study found that "employees indicate that improving workplace culture can improve retention. Sixty-two percent of all employees would have stayed if their company had taken steps to create a more positive and respectful work environment. Fifty-seven percent would have stayed if their company had taken steps to make the company culture more fair and inclusive." Talk about an opportunity for an inclusion dividend! Thus, uncovering and altering these patterns is imperative for leaders who wish to create inclusive organizations.

The work at the group level is threefold:

- To identify the group memberships that have an impact on the experiences of people in your organization.
- To uncover patterns related to those group memberships that are problematic, reducing engagement and productivity.

- To confront the insider–outsider dynamics that are creating or maintaining those patterns.

Work at the group level will complement the insights and skills emerging at the individual level.

The Level of Systems Framework is about creating real change that results in sustainable inclusion. So far, we've looked at the individual level, which is necessary and foundational but insufficient. We've looked at the group level, which is core to inclusion because the day-to-day work environment is most heavily impacted by the patterns and insider–outsider dynamics that exist at the group level. Work at the group level creates real change. However, to get sustainable change, there must be shifts at the organizational level as well.

The Organizational Level of Change

We think of the organizational level as the place where dynamics, norms, and practices are set into something just short of cement. Perhaps not quite superglue, something more like Elmer's glue. In other words, the organizational level is harder to change than the others, although certainly not impossible. We previously spoke of Korean Air having one of the worst safety records for decades. Although the company was flying modern aircraft, Korean cultural norms created conflict between a strict hierarchal organization and technology built for coordination between equals. Considering there are only a few main producers of aircraft and thousands of cultural systems, culture change had to match the technology instead of the other way around. The airline was able to unglue its pilots' adherence to hierarchical norms and now has one of the best safety records in the industry.

At the organizational level, the work of inclusion is about changing policies, processes, formal and informal norms, and the underlying assumptions that drive behavior in the organization. Thus, to some extent, it is about changing the culture of an organization, in that the culture often creates the informal norms and unwritten rules that become embedded. Here are some examples that describe these factors in more detail.

Policies and Practices

The work of inclusion at the organizational level involves uncovering and either dismantling or reducing the impact of policies that have unintended impacts. Sometimes these are little policies or practices that don't seem like a big deal. Here is an example. One organization we worked with had a push to drive down travel expenses. One easy target was premium parking at airports. A policy was put in place requiring all employees to use the economy lot. If you have been to a major airport recently, you probably let out a big sigh just now reading about this policy. Economy parking tends to be in distant, dark lots and requires a shuttle bus to get to the airport, increasing the time you spend on travel pre- and post-flight.

Instead of seeing a decrease in travel expenses, the company started to see it creep up for some employees while for others it dropped off altogether. During one of our sessions with the client the topic came up, and we quickly discovered that female employees were spending an extra day on travel so they could return in the morning instead of the dark of night. They did not want to trek out to an isolated parking area at a late hour. In addition, disabled employees found managing the buses and massive parking lots a huge physical challenge, prompting them to forgo travel that may have moved the company forward. An inclusive lens was soon added to all travel policy decisions. For this particular policy, the company simply added the line, "We trust employees will make the best decision with regard to this policy when it comes to their safety or physical limitations."

While this example may seem small in the bigger landscape of corporate policies and practices, consider the following typical corporate policies/ practices that may limit inclusion:

Recruitment Process

We've already spoken about how simply requiring a diverse interviewing team creates a more inclusive approach. Something as simple as a smartly worded job description can go a long way toward this goal as well. We once worked with the real estate management department of a large financial services company. The department was responsible for, among other things, managing the company's properties.

In the course of our work with the department managers, they identified the position of "project manager" as one that they wished to fill with a more diverse group of employees. They didn't understand why the position kept getting filled by middle-aged white men, while their overall workforce was getting more diverse. They were eager to find qualified candidates who didn't fall into the same demographic groups. Upon reviewing the position description, we realized that the problem might be the criteria used to screen candidates. Some of the criteria were twenty years old and reflected an outdated model of real estate management, from a time when such positions were filled mostly by white men. There was a new set of skills that was important for the job, and that would better position the project manager (a critical role in the organization) for higher-level jobs. Thus, the organization was able to both attract a more diverse set of candidates and better leverage its internal workforce for higher-level jobs.

Career Development and Promotion

The process of developing a pipeline of future leaders is multifaceted and occurs over many years. The potential for unconscious bias to impact this process is significant. Such bias shows up in informal ways, such as relationship building, networking, informal feedback, coaching and casual mentoring, visibility with clients and senior managers, and myriad other ways. It also shows up formally in terms of talent reviews and nine-box talent rating meetings, performance appraisals, succession planning, promotion decisions, training and development opportunities, and other organizationally sponsored and sanctioned activities. In all of these processes there is a potential for unintended bias—for notions of a "good fit"—to be the deciding factor in an increasingly competitive process as the pyramid narrows.

Company Networking and Entertainment Events

Most organizations hold events to celebrate success, build teams, and entertain clients. Quite often, these events are rooted in company history and tradition. They were created by and for a limited group of people, typically middle-aged, white, heterosexual men. As organizations have become more diverse, these events are proving problematic. Is sponsorship of a golf tournament the best or only way to build client relationships in this day and age? Do employee networking events always need to be after hours and involve alcohol? What are some team building events that truly include everyone?

Dress and Appearance

Many companies have a dress code. It is important to review these policies through a D&I lens. Does the dress code prohibit hats or require suits? Would you see an issue with religions that require head covering or age groups where suits are not fashionable? Whose standards are the codes based on? Do those standards still make sense today? What is the impact on customers? Which groups of people might be most affected by these policies? How do they affect the company brand? How do they impact the ability to recruit the best people? These are all important questions to ask if the goal is to create inclusion.

Family-Related Policies

Most organizations have a host of policies related to employees' family lives. These policies often speak to creating a workable balance between personal and professional lives, and they have evolved quite a bit in recent years to be more inclusive of all employees. The topic has become so critical that we have written an entire book on the subject, *The Golden Apple: Redefining Work-Life Balance for a Diverse Workforce*. Some organizations have broadened their definition of "family" so that policies are more inclusive of many types of families, including single-parent families, unmarried couples, same-sex couples, and so on. Corporations are providing parental leave benefits for both parents, as well as extending this policy to parents adopting a child. When these policies are inclusive, diverse groups of employees are more likely to be fully engaged. Employees who feel a sense of belonging have longer-term loyalty and are more engaged.

These are a few good examples of the way policies can be at odds with inclusion, though they are not intentionally set up to be inequitable. Given the right approach, management can create policies that consider the entire employee population while still reaching the overall policy goal.

Formal and Informal Behavioral Norms

Sometimes little norms have big impacts. An organization that we were tangentially involved with was examining its culture and looking for ways to create more inclusive norms. It was discovered that in one large division there was a norm of scheduling meetings early in the morning, as early as seven a.m. This is a norm that had evolved over time, with the intent of creating opportunities for collegial thinking at a quiet time of the day. In many ways, it made sense. These meetings had become increasingly important, and were a major source of information, both on and off the record.

When examined through an inclusion lens, however, it became apparent that this practice of early meetings advantaged some groups and disadvantaged others. You can probably begin to imagine those groups now. Women, who more frequently had child care responsibilities, were often unable to make the meetings. Commuters dependent upon public transportation found it challenging. New parents were also disadvantaged by this norm. There was a socioeconomic issue at play here as well, to the extent that some team members found it harder to afford extra child care. Single parents were disadvantaged by this norm. The team that uncovered this norm was quite amazed by the impact it was having, particularly because it was driven by positive intent, by the desire to create more productivity. However, these critical early meetings were creating insiders and outsiders, and were directly affecting the ability of some employees to develop and get promoted.

Images of Leadership

The notion of what makes a good leader is subtle and nuanced. It is often inherent in both national, regional, and organizational culture. Some organizations we have worked with have a notion of "gravitas." They say that to be a leader in their organization a person must have gravitas. Merriam-Webster's online dictionary defines gravitas as "high seriousness (as in a person's bearing on a subject)." Here is the problem: what is viewed as gravitas? It is a very subjective judgment. It is culturally based and extremely influenced by unconscious bias. We have heard literally hundreds of corporate women describe the phenomenon of taking a serious tone and having it be seen as aggressive, while watching their male colleagues exhibit the same behavior and have it seen as strong leadership. We have seen high-achieving leaders in East Asian regional offices perceived as mediocre at headquarters in New York or London, and passed over for larger global leadership roles. This perception seems to follow from the belief that these leaders' low-key leadership style isn't strong enough. Perceptions of gravitas might say more about the viewer of the behavior and/or the culture of the organization than about the individual being observed. These images of effective leadership must be discussed, made explicit, and examined for relevance and bias, or they will become unconsciously embedded into organizational culture and have profound and non-inclusive impacts on key talent-related decisions.

Culture

Ultimately, culture includes all of the little and not so little things that influence people to behave the way they do in an organization. Sometimes it is explicit (expressed in verbal or written form), sometimes implicit (expected, but not verbalized). We experience these cultural nuances in our daily lives. Would you show up at a longtime friend's house without calling first? How about someone you met only once? What time of day is it okay to call someone else's home? Did the person tell you explicitly to call within set times or was it simply inferred by the cultural norms that surround you? How would you express disagreement with a neighbor? Directly or in more subtle ways? What is an appropriate way to ask for assistance? How do you communicate your successes or failures? The list goes on and on. All of these questions translate into unwritten organizational or social norms. The extent to which an individual understands and behaves consistently with these norms will have an important impact on his ability to be successful. Laura Liswood, senior advisor at Goldman Sachs, speaks in her book *The Loudest Duck* about these norms, or "grandmas," as she calls them. She writes, "as we enter the workplace, we bring Grandma with us." Organizations have grandmas too, and these norms show up in the culture and are slow to change.

Culture often becomes apparent when there is an inconsistency between the implicit and the explicit. For example, many organizations go through extensive processes to identify values and behaviors that they want to be exhibited by their employees. In one of our client organizations, "courage" is one of the articulated values. However, very few employees were completely candid with managers and those above them in the hierarchy, even in situations that add significant risk or cost to the bottom line. What is being implicitly expressed that stops employees from following the explicit value? In our global environment, corporations find inconsistencies across boundaries when they explicitly impose a corporate "value" without considering the implicit cultural rules.

An inclusion initiative needs to impact the culture to some extent; it does not, however, have to achieve a complete culture change. The culture in many organizations is built for and favors certain groups. These are typically the groups that created the culture. New norms need to be created that work for a more diverse group of employees. In many organizations, simply engaging in D&I work at a level of depth is a start at changing the culture. There's an implicit norm in many organizations to not raise difficult or controversial issues. How can an organization make any progress on diversity and inclusion, both of which can be difficult and controversial, if employees don't feel they can speak candidly? Creating real and sustainable change requires some shifts at the organizational level. This can feel difficult. Thus, many organizations get stuck and take the easy way out. We will describe what sustainable change strategies look like in more detail in chapter 9.

Following are signs that your organization might be taking the easy way out and not creating a real and sustainable inclusion change initiative:

- There are a lot of diversity events, without any clear connection to the organization's business; this is a "diversity as PR" approach.
- Diversity conversations focus primarily on sharing global cuisine and simple cultural practices.
- Most of the efforts focus on outsider/minority groups and avoid full engagement of insider/majority groups, the groups who hold the most power and thus the greatest potential for breakthrough change.
- Inclusion development is done only at headquarters or only at a particular level of leadership.
- There is no visible, consistent senior leadership of the initiative (a statement by the CEO is not enough) the C-suite must be actively engaged in this complicated organizational change initiative, as the executives' understanding of how the organization works will be critical to developing the best strategies—of course, they also have to be believable role models.

What is the impact of all of this? If organizations don't create change at the organizational level, the impact can be substantial and may include:

- Lower levels of engagement, which can impact productivity and retention.
- Less access to relationship building and networking with clients and senior leaders.
- A decrease in team building.
- Less synergy.
- Lower levels of innovation.

- Creation of a closed negative feedback loop, where the organization keeps creating the same outcomes and limits its ability to grow.

The Marketplace Level of Change

All organizations exist for a reason. It may be profit or some social cause. All have stakeholders and customers/clients. The point at which the organization engages its stakeholders and client or consumer marketplace is a visible and critical boundary. It is directly related to the bottom line. We discussed the business case in detail in chapter 2, demonstrating the substantial impact of D&I. At this level of system there are four main areas of focus:

1. The organization's brand in the marketplace.
2. The extent to which an organization's staff reflects its customer base.
3. The ability to leverage D&I to create product and service breakthroughs.
4. The skill of customer-facing staff in engaging customers in an inclusive manner.

The fourth of these is often overlooked, yet for organizations that have a lot of contact with clients, customers, and communities, it is perhaps the most important of the four. If your employees fail to show up with a high level of skill and awareness about difference, you will lose business opportunities.

One of our colleagues distinctly remembers being visited by a financial advisor early in his career. The advisor requested the meeting and came to his home. The advisor wanted to talk, as did our colleague, about financial goals over the long term and about how to start investing.

When our colleague mentioned his partner (who was male), the fact didn't seem to register. The advisor wasn't really able to talk about the financial planning needs unique to those in same-sex relationships. He didn't seem prepared or comfortable. He did not get our colleague's business. These sorts of interactions happen all the time. Bump this up to a higher level and imagine a team from a Big Four accounting firm or a large financial services firm engaging with the team of a current or potential client. How do they show up to that client? How do they interact with the client team? If a woman leads the client team, do they treat her as the lead, or do they unconsciously treat one of the male team members as the lead? If there is a generational difference, how well do they manage it?

The Underlying Issue Is Power

The Levels of Systems Framework we have been describing is primarily about power. Power increases when we get broader than the individual level. At the individual level, our power is limited. For example, as we will discuss in chapter 5, which deals with unconscious bias, individuals are equal in their ability to be biased. However, our ability to affect the lives of other people in substantial ways increases when we get to the group level. When bias is expressed at the group level, as a pattern, it can affect large numbers of people in their ability to have full access to opportunity. An obvious example of this is housing discrimination. When a white person and a person of color are living next to each other, both are equally capable of being biased against the other. They may or may not choose to act on that bias. Except in extreme cases, they are not able to significantly impact the other's ability to live freely and pursue happiness. However, if I am part of a group that carries a bias **and** has the power to implement that bias on a broader scale, then we can significantly affect the lives of another group.

In the United States, such bias showed up as housing discrimination, when white people limited where people of color could live. It showed up as limits on the financial independence of women. It showed up as restrictions on lesbian, gay, and bisexual people's ability to live full lives. How might this show up today, in a large organization?

There is a good chance that group-level bias will show up in ways that are not intended to create inequality. Remember, intent is not required for bias to have a negative effect. If male managers are comfortable with one another, share a lot in common, and build a good rapport, this will likely have a positive impact on the group's ability to work together. A female manager in that group might have a harder time building those relationships and being seen as credible. Perhaps a group of baby boomer managers is able to crowd out the opinion of a younger employee, invoking more substantial experience.

Group-level bias, though, is at its most powerful when it is institutionalized through formal and informal policies, practices, and laws. Thus, there is even more power at the organizational level, the level at which bias can be "baked into the cake," so to speak. Most organizations are driven by their mission. The mission is almost always about the clients and customers. Power increases at the marketplace level because an organization's activities are meaningless if they aren't connecting to clients and customers effectively.

An organization that connects its inclusion efforts to the marketplace will differentiate itself from its peers. The framework is offered as a guide to do just that. The first step is to begin asking some critical questions (see figure 4-2).

The leadership challenge and opportunity are substantial here (more on leadership in chapter 8). The fundamental leadership challenge is, at some level, to see outside of our own box. The inherent dilemma is that the higher we are in leadership, the more likely it is that we have a lot of important "insider" group memberships. These memberships affect our worldview. The bottom line is, when we are in an insider group, we tend to not see the insider–outsider dynamics. As insiders, we may be leading with good intent but missing a critical piece of the picture. Just asking the questions posed above in figure 4-2 is an act of leadership. The Levels of System Framework is a leadership tool that can help us frame the inclusion work in a way that goes beyond our own knowledge base.

Individual	Group/Team	Organization	Marketplace
• What is the awareness and skill of our managers and staff? • Are our leaders effective role models of inclusive behavior?	• What group level patterns exist in the organization? • Which group memberships are most important in our business? • How do insider–outsider dynamics impact team performance?	• What are the norms, written and unwritten? • How are we ensuring that our people processes are objective? • What is our internal brand?	• Are we engaging our clients inclusively? • What is our external brand? • Are we leveraging inclusion to grow our business?

FIGURE 4-2 Levels of Systems Questions

Takeaways

- ✓ There are four levels of systems that influence an inclusive environment: individual, group, organization, and marketplace.
- ✓ The most difficult, yet most powerful, system to change is the one at the organizational level.
- ✓ The most critical day-to-day dynamics of inclusion occur at the group level, as employees interact with one another individually and on teams.

✓ Individual-level and leadership development alone does not create sustainable change. Such development must be combined with a strategic approach that incorporates all levels of systems.

✓ Policies, practices, and implicit and explicit norms can have a significant impact on acquiring, retaining, and leveraging a diverse and inclusive workforce. It is important to get beyond the intent of these policies and to examine their impact through a D&I lens.

Discussion Point

YourMoney Inc. is a large financial services firm with financial advisors located in major cities across the globe. The marketing team has uncovered an emerging trend within the industry. Women are independently making more financial decisions about matters such as 401k rollovers and mutual fund and mortgage firm selections. Marketing presented this trend to the executive sales team. One member of the team thought it was a fad. Another wanted Marketing to recheck their numbers and sources. The majority accepted what Marketing had to offer but did not see a need for systemic change, though 76 percent of the company's advisors were male. After all, their leading male financial advisors had female clients. One of the executives noted, "Traditionally, men held the role of making financial decisions in the household, so women would be inclined to listen more to a male advisor." The resulting action was to put more women in the company's ads and to provide some training for male advisors on how to better approach this growing demographic.

Using the Level of Systems Framework as a tool, how would you answer the following questions:

◆ What are the challenges and opportunities at the individual level when we think about the role of financial advisor?

♦ What group-level patterns and insider–outsider dynamics could be influencing the internal debate between marketing and the executive team?

♦ How might the policies and practices of the organization be having an impact? What about the impact of written and unwritten norms? The culture of the company?

♦ What are the marketplace implications of this situation?

5

Unconscious and Unintentional Bias

Mark vividly recalls a conversation with a senior-level hiring manager, Phil, who leads a sales team. The company where Phil worked was very profitable and was located in a part of the country that was quite diverse in terms of race, gender, ethnicity, sexual orientation, and age. Mark was working on a project to increase the sales division's ability to acquire and develop more diverse talent and a more diverse customer base. Phil was resistant, however; he didn't feel it was necessary, felt business was good, and didn't see a lot of value to be unlocked by increasing the diversity of the talent pool and client base.

Mark and Phil had several meetings, at the urging of the divisional executive. Mark recalls vividly a conversation with Phil about how he screened potential hires. Phil said that his main criterion was whether he would feel comfortable with that candidate coming into his home with his wife and children. Mark was struck by the implications of what Phil was saying, and also grateful for his honesty. Mark didn't believe Phil truly understood the implications of this measure. He was defining both his talent pool and his customer base from his own biases. We should add that Phil had considerable wealth and was quite socially conservative in his views. It was a good bet that he did not have a very diverse guest list for gatherings at his house.

Instead of analyzing the best talent fit for the division's target market, Phil's hiring filter selected the best fit for a friend. He'd been successful for himself, his staff, and the business in the past. However, the company was growing and the demographics of its target audience were changing rapidly. Phil's behavior was causing the business to be poorly positioned for growth over the long term.

In this chapter, we will examine unconscious bias. We will review recent research from the fields of brain physiology, social psychology, and organizational psychology, all of which contribute to a much clearer picture of the role and impact of bias in organizations. This research has helped reframe the D&I conversation to one that is about accepting the reality of bias and moving toward creating awareness and systems that minimize the impact of bias on the structural, process, and human aspects of an organization.

We will also examine unconscious bias at the systemic level. As we discussed in an earlier chapter, it is easy to think of inclusion at the individual level, however that is limiting when it comes to organizational change. Bias gets embedded into all sorts of organizational systems and processes. It also affects how an organization views and engages its marketplace.

Following are key points that we will cover in this chapter:

- Unconscious bias is pervasive and universal.
- Unconscious bias translates into behaviors, often subtle and small, that can have big impacts on fairness and inclusiveness.
- While we are all equal in our capacity to be biased, the impact of bias is experienced differently for different groups.
- Unconscious bias goes beyond the individual level and becomes embedded systemically.

- Unconscious bias impacts the ability of an organization to fully engage its marketplace.
- Unconscious bias can be ameliorated or reduced at both the individual and the systems level.

Please know there is a substantial amount of research in this area. We are not going to overwhelm you with research, but will instead pull out the themes and findings that have the most practical value to you as leaders. We are most interested in how this research changes the D&I conversation in important ways.

Changing the D&I Conversation

The diversity and inclusion conversation has always been a challenging one. At a very basic level, it invites self- and organizational reflection. It requires acceptance of the possibility that the playing field is not level and something needs to change. For many, this introspection creates guilt and defensiveness. All of this is wrapped up in the provocative and contentious historical context of human rights movements. Thus, the D&I conversation is challenging in the following ways:

- There is resistance (particularly among "insider" groups) to the idea that discriminatory behavior is happening, because many believe this means it must be happening intentionally.
- It has focused primarily on the bad behaviors of white, heterosexual men.
- It taps defensiveness, which is born out of cognitive dissonance created when well-intentioned people are asked to accept that they are treating others unfairly or that they are benefitting from systemic advantages.

- It challenges a deep belief in many countries and cultures in fairness and equity; to challenge that is to run up against deeply held values.

Many people believe in meritocracy, a system in which the best, most capable people get ahead because of their abilities and skills. Quite often, a belief in meritocracy is paired with a belief that it has largely been achieved. Challenging that idea means challenging an entire belief system. Most don't like thinking that they are a part of and are contributing to an unfair system. It is dissonant with personal and societal values of fairness and equal opportunity. This is an undercurrent in much of the D&I work of the last thirty years.

Much D&I work has been polarized into two camps: the first camp says that we should focus squarely and sharply on the privilege of majority or dominant groups, particularly white people and men. Making sure that these groups "get it" is of primary importance. The other camp says that we need to make diversity about everything and everybody, and not focus on power or privilege. From this perspective, keeping all groups involved and comfortable is of primary importance.

Our view leans toward the first camp but doesn't ignore some truths brought forth by the second. The truth, in our view, lies somewhere else (not quite in between), and pulls from each of these perspectives. It is hard to deny that power and privilege often arise based on factors such as race, gender, culture, class, sexual orientation, etc. It does no good to avoid talking about this rather large elephant in the room, just to keep people comfortable. On the other hand, it is important to do this in a way that is productive and doesn't alienate key decision makers. It is import-ant to distinguish where we truly are all equal as human beings, and it is important to not alienate those in power, many of whom are well inten-tioned and want inclusion and meritocracy. We think the recent work on unconscious bias allows for a real and serious engagement of the issues and preserves respect for individuals' basic integrity.

As we have been saying, one of the biggest challenges in creating real and sustainable inclusion has been overcoming the guilt and defensiveness that the conversation provokes, particularly among members of insider groups. Let's look at this more closely. The notion that there is substantial inequality can be difficult to stomach for people who believe in freedom and opportunity. At the individual level, this creates guilt and defensiveness, neither of which are great spurs for change. In fact, what is created is disengagement and defense of the status quo. Essentially, most of us don't like to acknowledge our own biases and shortcomings. We don't want to consider or acknowledge that bias may have operated in our favor. While some people are open to the fact that unfairness and inequity exists in a larger sense, when they look at inequalities at the individual level they experience cognitive dissonance.

Cognitive dissonance, a theory developed by Leon Festinger, is the discomfort caused by trying to hold two ideas (cognitions) at the same time. Festinger proposes that people have a motivational drive to reduce dissonance by altering existing cognitions or adding new ones to create consistency. You can imagine that the notion that we might be actively biased is a nonstarter, primarily because it challenges our self-image. Thus, the subtext of many D&I conversations and workshops is something like this: "Are you trying to tell me that I am a racist/sexist/homophobe? That's not how I perceive myself and in fact it is inconsistent with my values. I treat all people fairly." With discussions on unconscious bias, a defensive conversation can be avoided or engaged in a more empowering way.

Some of the Latest Research on Unconscious Bias

Several streams of research on unconscious bias are converging to change the D&I conversation in important ways. This research pulls from the neurosciences, social psychology and organizational dynamics, and even economic decision making. Substantial work has been done at Harvard University with Project Implicit, an educational research and resource on bias. Mahzarin Benaji (a psychologist at Harvard University), Anthony Greenwald (a professor of psychology at University of Washington), and Brian Nosek (a professor of psychology at University of Virginia) have done considerable research and created a groundbreaking test for implicit bias. Their project and its related research bring these streams together and have demonstrated that:

- Bias is ever present, unavoidable, and human. Even when the intention is to be inclusive, as it often is, the perceptions that sit in the unconscious brain often rule the day when it comes to decision-making. This process happens quickly, much more quickly than the process of conscious reasoning.
- Bias translates into behavior. There are numerous examples of bias translating into behavior, both at the interpersonal level (interactions) and the systems level (processes), from first impressions to hiring decisions to performance evaluations and promotions. It is impossible to separate bias from behavior unless that bias is made conscious.
- Bias affects performance. Not only does bias result in less than optimal decisions, it also affects performance in a more indirect way. A large body of research on the Pygmalion effect and self-fulfilling prophecy has demonstrated that leaders' perceptions and expectations directly affect the performance of their staff.

Let's look at each of these general findings in more detail.

Bias Is Ever Present, Unavoidable, and Human

All human beings are biased. That includes us and that includes you. We are biased because we have to be. We are exposed to incredible amounts of information from multiple sources. Our conscious brain simply cannot make sense of all of that information in a way that allows us to function in our busy and complicated world, which leads us to take shortcuts. These shortcuts primarily involve categorizing and priming. Think of the unconscious brain, or old brain, or primal brain, as a computer hard drive. On that hard drive is stored an incredible amount of information, way too much for us to keep track of consciously. Thus, we tap that information often unknowingly, without conscious thought. This allows us to make quick decisions.

We work with leaders who are constantly making judgments and decisions. They are busy and their work is complicated. They have to rely on their gut instincts quite regularly. The good news is that they, and we as human beings, are remarkably good at this process. Malcolm Gladwell, in his groundbreaking book *Blink,* describes the phenomenon of "thin-slicing," where we are able to make accurate decisions with very little conscious data. We can do this because we are tapping the stored data on the hard drive in our unconscious brain. As Gladwell points out, we do this very rapidly. Gladwell gives strong testimony to our success in making quick judgments. Think about yourself. How many decisions do you make in a day that are conscious and thoughtful?

Daniel Kahneman, in his book *Thinking, Fast and Slow,* identifies System 1 and System 2 thinking. System 1 thinking is the quick, automatic judgments and decisions that we make without conscious thought. System 2 thinking involves those decisions that we make consciously and intentionally. His research reveals that more than 90 percent of our decisions are System 1. Kahneman agrees with Gladwell that many of our System 1 judgments and decisions are accurate. Your daily commute home often does not require intense decision-making. How many of us have arrived home and realized we were on autopilot almost the entire way? Now, think about visiting a foreign country where drivers use the opposite side of the road and entering a rotary. The new challenge requires you to engage your System 2 thinking. In our view, certain talent acquisition and management decisions create challenges that should be addressed by System 2.

Unfortunately, when it comes to people judgments, or, more formally in a work context, talent acquisition and talent management, the data on our brain's hard drive is frequently full of stereotypes and misinformation. These are the result of messages received from many sources throughout our lives. Many of us reject these old stereotypes—in our conscious brain, we don't believe them any longer. The problem lies in our unconscious brain, where the messages remain and inform our perceptions, judgments, and behavior. "But wait!" you might be thinking, "I really, really don't believe those old stereotypes." Again, that is your conscious brain talking. Old stereotypes are continually reinforced in ways that don't allow us to truly change the information on the hard drive. The most effective way to change the data sitting on the hard drive is to get new data. This requires new experiences, on a regular basis, with people who are different from us.

When Raul entered the workforce, he felt very strongly that men and women were equally capable and were deserving of equal rights. That was (and still is) his conscious belief. However, much of his unconscious brain's hard drive data and experiences presumed that men are the expected leaders in the workplace. He grew up in a family in which all of the men worked outside the home and the vast majority of the women worked inside the home. He grew up in a community where the same thing was true. He watched TV and read books that reinforced the same messages. That is a lot of data. Yet still, he consciously believed in gender equality.

In his first job, Raul was soon being supervised by a woman. She was a competent professional, seasoned in her field, and someone from whom he was expected to learn. Consciously, he was delighted to have her as his leader. Unconsciously, though, he had a hard time seeing her as a leader in the business world. Raul distinctly remembers her telling him one day in her office that he needed to stop treating her as if she was his mother. It takes a long time to shift those sorts of unconsciously held biases. Over the years, he has been on work teams led by women. He has worked with many women as peers. Those experiences have been added to his unconscious brain's hard drive, and it is now much more likely that he will behave consistent with his consciously held values and beliefs about women and men in the workplace.

Bias Translates into Behavior

We don't just make assumptions and judgments. We act on them in ways that impact people, processes, and organizations. Earlier in the book, we discussed research on names done by Marianne Bertrand, professor at the Chicago Graduate School of Business, and Sendhil Mullainathan, professor at MIT. Their experiment was designed to determine whether employers were discriminating against job applicants with African American–sounding names. Bertrand and Mullainathan sent out nearly five thousand résumés for thirteen hundred job openings in Chicago and Boston. Every employer received résumés for four types of applicant: an average Caucasian applicant, an average African American applicant, a highly skilled Caucasian applicant, and a highly skilled African American applicant. The study found that applicants with "Caucasian-sounding names" were 50 percent more likely to get an interview than applicants with "African American–sounding" names. They also found that lower-skilled Caucasian applicants received more interviews than highly skilled African American applicants.

The study revealed that employers have an unconscious bias against African American–sounding names, which causes them to react negatively toward those applicants' résumés. It is important to note that most of these companies stated that they were actively seeking diversity in their candidate pools. The results seem illogical, but this is how unconscious bias works. We cite this piece of research because it has such obvious and important implications for organizations that wish to become more diverse and inclusive. There are many other studies showing essentially the same thing. For example, until blind auditions were implemented, orchestras overwhelmingly hired men. Taller men earn, on average, about $800 more a year per inch of height from five feet seven inches to six foot three inches.

We believe there are three kinds of bias that result in non-inclusive behavior:

- Priming: Organizations are social systems. We rely on one another for information. When a trusted colleague thinks highly of another colleague or a potential hire, I am more likely to feel similarly. We are easily "primed" to feel positively or negatively toward another person.

- Affinity bias: Most of us can relate more easily to people who share similar backgrounds or experiences. Often, we feel a higher level of comfort with those like us. Almost certainly, we can more easily empathize with those we have an "affinity" for. Affinity bias can create a sort of halo effect.

- Confirmation bias/stereotyping: Stereotypes are rampant in our diverse society. Many of us do not consciously believe many of these stereotypes, but they are stored in our unconscious brain nonetheless. If a person does something that fits our stereotype, it tends to confirm and strengthen that stereotype.

All of these create first impressions—the extent to which we have an immediately positive or negative impression of an individual. First impressions tend to be enduring, particularly in the workplace, where time is short and "fit" is often considered important. First impressions are formed within seconds or minutes, are directly connected to our comfort level, and can profoundly impact interactions and decisions.

Bias Affects Performance

There is no longer a need to debate whether or not we are biased. That question has been answered strongly in the affirmative. It is time to turn the conversation to the implications of those biases, as there are many for leaders who are working toward meritocracy and inclusion.

Organizations are obviously concerned about fairness. However, they are likely even more concerned about performance. It is clear that unconscious bias impacts performance in several ways:

- Bias influences the decisions that leaders make, leading to inaccurate ratings of merit and thus to less than ideal talent management decisions.
- Bias creates expectations, and a leader's expectations have a direct impact on performance.
- Bias, via stereotypes, can create lower performance among members of outsider groups, or among groups that have negative stereotypes associated with them.

Many of us may vaguely remember the "self-fulfilling prophecy," or Pygmalion effect, from our Psych 101 class. This well-replicated phenomenon shows how the expectations of people in positions of power directly and powerfully affect the behavior and performance of those subordinate to them. Thus bias, consciously or unconsciously held, directly impacts the performance of team members. Social psychologist Claude Steele's research shows how this effect is amplified in the context of well-established historic stereotypes. Steele and his colleagues researched and described something called "stereotype threat." This effect serves to reduce the performance of individuals within a group in situations where the stereotype is applicable. For example, if women are reminded of their gender prior to a test of their math and science skills, they will underperform compared with a group of women not reminded of their gender. This is because of the stereotype that women are less capable in math and science than men are.

Similar effects were found for racial and ethnic minority groups. This obviously has implications for leaders who are working to create an environment where stereotype threat is reduced, and it is particularly important as groups begin to occupy nontraditional roles. In science and technology, for example, more women are entering the field, despite strongly held societal stereotypes about women being less capable in scientific or technological pursuits.

Equal Capacity for Bias, Different Impacts

The vast majority of human beings are biased, for all of the reasons enumerated above. This is the place we are all equal, and our group identities don't make a difference. You will remember this as the individual level of the Level of Systems Framework. White people, for example, aren't necessarily any more biased than people of color. This should be reassuring to some, who feel that diversity and inclusion work suggests that some individuals are better than others in terms of their level of bias. Again, we are all equal, and the work of diversity and inclusion is not about good or bad individuals. The impact of bias, however, is not equal. The biases of insider groups are generally the biases that carry the day, have more "oomph," and get institutionalized at the organization level. They become systemic biases, which means they have broader impact. Biases can bestow an unearned positive or negative characteristic, depending on your group membership.

As an example: because men hold a disproportionate number of leadership positions, and the percentage was even higher in the past, the image of good leadership is often based on typical male leadership styles. Men and women are socialized differently. They are taught to behave, and to lead, in different ways. If the image of good leadership is based on typical male behaviors, then many women will find it hard to be seen as good leaders and get promoted into leadership positions. In one organization we work with, executives describe how they want leaders to have "presence." When we ask them to describe what a person with "presence" looks like (we ask them to do this quickly, without thinking), the description is almost always of a tall man in a dark suit with short hair and glasses. It is not hard to see the implicit or unconscious bias present in this image. It is also not hard to see the systemic impact. Organizations pay a price for this, because research on leadership, particularly the recent work on emotional intelligence, suggests that behaviors women are socialized to use are effective and underutilized in many organizations.

Systemic Bias

Unconscious bias is frequently understood as a primarily psychological, inter- and intra-personal phenomenon. Perhaps its biggest impact, though, is on institutions and organizations. We define systemic bias as bias, conscious or unconscious, that gets institutionalized through policies, practices, and culture. Some systemic biases are appropriate and helpful. For example, a bank known as being conservative in extending credit was biased toward organizations that met a high standard of credit worthiness. This bias affected many of its decisions. During the banking crisis of the late 1980s, this was a useful bias, as the organization emerged from the crisis unscathed. We are concerned with a different kind of systemic bias, the kind that affects talent acquisition and talent management functions. Systemic bias occurs when:

1. **The biases of very powerful individuals get magnified.** A company we are familiar with has a preponderance of executives who graduated from one particular university. These executives also share other similarities. The top executive went to the same university. It seems farfetched to think that the most competent candidates for executive positions just happened to come from the same university, especially considering that the organization did not require a specific skill set that one might find more at one university than another.

It is clear that there is a bias that emanates from the preferences of the top executive. Because of his position and power, his individual bias has an outsized, systemic impact. If we asked him (and we haven't), he might defend his personnel decisions and state with certainty that he picked the most qualified and appropriate candidates for these positions. Indeed, the executives might be quite competent but, stepping back from each individual decision, it is clear that there is a pattern, and indeed a bias, at play. The bias is likely systemic in that it affects not just one decision but a series of decisions. We suspect the bias starts in the screening process, perhaps reflected in the position description, and is at play when interviewers are prepped about candidates. It also shows up in the discussions assessing candidates. This bias likely also affects the informal networking, rapport building, and social interaction usually critical to executive career development. In performance appraisals and promotion decisions, this bias likely appears.

2. **A bias becomes part of a process or system, usually unintentionally.** There are a number of ways that biases are incorporated into a process, including the following:

- An old rating in a performance review from a biased manager rules an employee out of a promotion.
- An unequal pay policy persists, as it set some employees' salaries at lower levels initially.
- A team of reviewers for promotion decisions are almost exclusively from similar backgrounds; this affects their view of candidates who do not fit that background. Prior to the promotion discussion, their rapport and level of comfort is higher with candidates who are like them; there is a cumulative effect, and their decisions are viewed as appropriate because they were made not by an individual but by a team.

3. **A bias based in the historical culture of an organization continues to have an impact.** One organization we worked with had a warehouse position that required the worker to move large blocks of product. There had never been a woman working in this job because it was assumed that the job required heavy lifting and therefore was not appropriate for women. Senior management (under pressure) decided to begin hiring women. Lo and behold, gender wasn't a valid criterion. The job was quickly evolving to one in which heavy lifting was less important, a change that was good for the organization because the number of disability claims was high when strenuous lifting was required. The change wasn't, however, reflected in the job description and interview criteria. Incidentally, the addition of women into the job was extremely successful and resulted in a faster transition to techniques that did not require heavy lifting to move the product. The reduction of disability claims continued, and the company almost doubled its recruitment pool.

In a similar example, we have frequently heard about IBM's strict dress policy of dark suits and ties. This policy extended well back into the company's history and was probably based at one time in a solid business case related to the company's brand identity and desire to present a professional impression with clients. When the company began to hire women into professional and managerial jobs, the policy created a dilemma for women, who began to wear dark suits and ties to fit in to the company culture. An entirely new wardrobe of "professional" dress for women was created based on the need to fit in. Ultimately, IBM changed its policy so that women could both look professional and feel comfortable at work.

To root out this kind of bias, organizations need to look at the most critical positions and ask questions about the true skills required to perform those functions. This process is a "win" all the way around. It results in a clearer set of skill needs and performance expectations, and it will also either improve or expand (or both) the talent pool. Ultimately, while bias is reduced, performance and productivity are raised. But it's important to not throw the proverbial baby out with the bath water: an organization needs to retain the parts of its culture that really make a difference while letting go of those aspects that are based in bias.

Taking Advantage of Neuroplasticity: Reducing Unconscious Bias

It is challenging to try to change behaviors that are unconscious. Obviously, the first step is making the unconscious conscious, not an easy task for most of us. There is another difficulty. Unconscious bias feeds on itself in a sort of negative reinforcing cycle. Once an idea, notion, perception, etc. is set in our old (unconscious) brain, it operates outside our awareness most of the time. It has a domino effect, as we behave consistently with that perception, impact others based on our bias, and reinforce their negative experiences. This serves to continually reinforce our biases, and our behavior can evoke the behavior we expect to see in others. What do we mean by this?

There is recent good news in the research on neuroplasticity. Defined simply as the ability of our brains to change throughout our lives, neuroplasticity means our brains can be wired and rewired for negative or positive outcomes. Behaviors are not written in stone but are formed over time. Given enough time and attention, they can be re-formed. If we are conscious of our biases, we can reprogram our brains by consciously changing our behavior. This can be done proactively or reactively.

Here is an example of neuroplasticity used in a positive way: Doris is a schoolteacher. She told us that whenever she took on a new class, she would intentionally not look at the standardized test scores of the students. She knew that she would expect more of the kids who had higher test scores and might miss the contributions of those who tested lower. She understood that knowledge of their test scores would create or reinforce biases she would find hard to control. The students would begin to respond to her expectations, and perform consistently with them. She demonstrates two important behaviors in reducing unconscious bias:

- Being open to the fact that she was likely biased and therefore increasing her self-awareness.
- Putting in place a process to ensure she wouldn't unintentionally treat her students in a biased way.

Looking at the following model (figure 5-1), it is critical to accept the first step in this model as a basic psychological and physiological fact: our brains operate in such a way that we will have biases. Many of these will be unconscious and unintentional, but they will be there nonetheless. If you take nothing more from this chapter, please accept this one fact. Because we can't easily change the basic physiology of our brains, we are left with three other points on this model where we can create change.

Because it is challenging to examine our own assumptions and behavior, we often find ourselves at the fourth point on this model, discussing or arguing about an inequitable impact. We tend to miss points two and three, although they are the places where we can have a real impact. A fairly substantial body of research indicates that we can alter our preformed expectations and assumptions. This is not easy work but it is valuable and doable. Essentially, we need to have a substantial number of experiences that counter those preformed assumptions. Some research done in conjunction with the Implicit Association Test (a demonstration test from Project Implicit) found that bias against black people could be reduced when subjects were exposed to pictures of important black historical figures. This effect was temporary, however.

If you are a leader in an organization, it is critical to expose yourself to and interact with people who are different from you. These individuals need to be your peers or have more experience or expertise than you. Do this regularly. It is also possible to alter or minimize the impact of your behavior, which is point three in this model. You will need to create ground rules for yourself and cultivate relationships with others who will give you feedback. Mark remembers with a mix of embarrassment and thankfulness a situation in which his unconscious gender bias was show-ing up in a meeting he was facilitating. Essentially, in a brainstorming ses-sion he was taking the men's opinions more seriously than the women's. Mark was not aware of this and it was certainly not his intent. Fortunately, he had a male colleague who was willing to give him feedback about his behavior. Without that feedback, Mark would not have known the impact of his behavior, and he might've damaged some key relationships.

We can also use neuroplasticity reactively. Mark remembers sitting on a plane that was rolling toward the runway and hearing a woman's voice come from the cockpit. For the first time he can remember, at least one of the pilots flying him was a woman. From the perspective of his conscious brain, Mark was not the least bit concerned about the gender of the pilot. He knew logically that the skill set pilots need is not gender based. However, his unconscious brain had a different idea. He was embarrassed to find that he felt uncomfortable when he heard her voice. This discomfort was about all the stereotypes in his unconscious brain, the stereotypes that had been embedded and reinforced since he was a child about the proper roles of men and women.

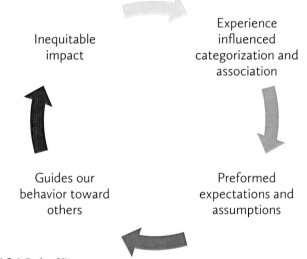

Inequitable impact

Experience influenced categorization and association

Guides our behavior toward others

Preformed expectations and assumptions

FIGURE 5-1 Cycle of Bias

Mark's experience did present an opportunity, though, for him to become proactive. He began to be as aware as possible, always looking into the cockpit to see who was flying the plane. He noticed that occasionally the pilots were women. Each time, his nervousness decreased, and after several such flights he had no noticeable reaction to the gender of the pilot. By proactively raising his awareness, Mark was taking advantage of neuroplasticity and rewiring his brain to accommodate new ideas about gender roles.

All of these ways of reducing unconscious bias come back to one thing: an ability to be open and challenge yourself. If you are reading this book, it is likely that you are willing to learn. Most successful organizational change efforts start with a leader looking in the mirror. Inclusion is no different.

In summary, there are some very tangible ways to reduce unconscious bias:

- Accept that you carry biases, that you are probably not aware of many of them, and that your good intentions are not enough to make them go away.
- Rewire your brain by regularly interacting with people who are different from you, both inside and outside of work. Read the work of authors who are different from you. Do this repeatedly and over time.
- Put process checks in place that will interrupt System 1 thinking for critical decision-making and prompt you and others to explicitly consider the possibility of bias during talent acquisition and talent management interactions and decisions. For example, before sitting down to conduct an interview ask yourself what bias you may carry (positive or negative) toward that individual and plan to minimize its impact.
- Develop peer coaching and feedback relationships that will enable you to get feedback from people who are different from you. Work hard to build sufficient trust that will enable honest feedback.
- Examine important talent acquisition and talent management processes and redesign them to minimize the potential impact of bias. When you are making critical decisions that impact

people and teams, ensure that there are "System 2 moments" in the process that interrupt the accumulation of unconscious bias. For example, require multi-source input that involves the input of a diverse group of colleagues when assessing employees' performance and potential.

Takeaways

- ✓ Unconscious bias is human.
- ✓ Three types of bias influence our behavior: priming, affinity, and confirmation.
- ✓ Our biases impact an organization's ability to fully leverage diversity.
- ✓ Biases can become embedded in processes and be systemic.
- ✓ Unconscious bias can be mitigated with conscious development.

Discussion Point

The scenario below summarizes a recruiter's effort to best manage the first round of résumé selection in a limited time. Karen is one of her company's most successful recruiters, handling an average of twenty-five requisitions per month, filling 75 percent of the positions within forty-five days. Read the scenario and answer the questions that follow.

Karen opened up her application folder for the financial analyst position. The number of résumés listed gave her a moment to sigh: 152 résumés have been submitted for this position. She had one hour before her next interview to disposition them all and send the five best to the hiring manager.

She had built a process for weeding through the résumés quickly. Her company had targeted five universities for their college recruitment program. Even though this was not a college hire, Karen knew that having attended the targeted college would give a candidate a leg up. She was able to quickly filter out with a quick Boolean search those who did not have one of these five colleges on their résumés. This process left her with a manageable thirty-two résumés. A quick review showed all but five had the prerequisites for the opening.

Karen knew the candidate for this position had to have sound mathematical skills. The last person hired for this position was Ann Sung. Kim Lee's résumé had similarities with Ann's, so it went into the best pile. "Only four more to go," Karen whispered to herself.

Candidates Sam Johnson and Fred Hanlon were both US Navy reservists, as was Peter, the hiring manager. Karen knew Peter would enjoy speaking with them. "Two résumés for the best pile left and fifteen minutes before I have to get going," she thought.

The company had recently created a requirement that all candidate pools have at least two "diversity" individuals. Although there were no photos on the résumés, Karen thought Jamal Williams was African American, so she added his résumé to the pool to help satisfy this requirement. Lastly, she saw a résumé of someone who had worked at her previous employer. She liked everyone she had interviewed from this employer, so this résumé helped her get to the five best, with five minutes to spare for a bathroom break.

- ◆ Where do you see possibilities for affinity, confirmation, and systemic bias?
- ◆ What could Karen do differently to limit the impact of some of her biases?
- ◆ How could the company change hiring practices to limit bias in the selection process?

6

Insider–Outsider Dynamics

This story is a compilation of many situations we have observed, uncovered in assessments, or heard from friends and family. For the past three months, Sarah has been going through the interviewing process with a civil engineering firm that has five hundred employees. The interview process was a bit grueling, with multiple behavioral interviews, personality testing, and subject matter testing. She was thrilled to finally get a call offering her the job. Although Sarah was certainly not the first woman at the firm, she was going to be its first female engineer. Sarah had always been a trailblazer and liked breaking new ground. She would have the chance to work alongside some great talent and be exposed to senior leadership as well as take on high-profile assignments. The firm had just won the bid to build a massive multiple bridge system connecting two highways in a major metropolitan area.

During interviews, Sarah had been asked several times if she could commit to a five-year project and whether she was "considering any life changes" that might not allow her to finish a long-term assignment. After the third time the question was asked by a different individual, she thought maybe the firm had an issue with people leaving in the middle of projects. One of her close friends was vying for the same job. When she mentioned the attention to this detail, he said it was only mentioned to him once, as an aside.

Sarah signed the hire paperwork and sent it back the very next day. After a week passed, she called to confirm receipt. She left a message with her new boss, but received a call back from HR. They said Paul, her new boss, was busy, but they wanted to let her know they received the paperwork. They provided Sarah a date and time for her to start.

She showed up to her new employer thirty minutes early, eager to start digging in. The last time she'd spoken to her new boss was three weeks previously, when he called to make the offer. She found her way to HR. They had some additional paperwork and showed Sarah to her office area. All of the civil engineers had offices, but Sarah was given a cubical because her future office had not yet been converted from a makeshift conference room. HR explained that Paul was off site for the morning but would be back around noon. Due to some communication error, her laptop was not going to be ready until the next day.

Sarah took the opportunity to go around the office and introduce herself to the new team. She first stopped by Frank's office. Frank beamed a smile, stood up and shook her hand warmly, and said, "So you are the one who helped us win the big contract." Sarah was a little confused, as she had not worked on a contract. There was some idle chat. Frank took the opportunity to introduce Sarah to Ramesh in the next office before he went back to his desk. Ramesh was cordial, but not as friendly as Frank. He asked if she was going to the Stanford University happy hour after work. Sarah explained she'd gone to MIT and not Stanford. Ramesh replied, "Wow, Paul actually hired somebody not from Stanford. Guess he is breaking all types of traditions." Sarah chuckled and quipped, "Well, once you let one MIT in, there is no stopping them." Ramesh gave a polite smile.

The remaining engineers were out of the office, so Sarah went back to her empty cube. The recruiter, Kristin, who'd first interviewed her stopped by to invite her to lunch. Sarah accepted and soon found herself being introduced to all of the other women in the office. Everyone was very welcoming. There were a few jokes about her joining the men's club. Kristin told Sarah she was a big win because the firm was required to increase gender diversity on the team as part of the bid conditions.

Paul called Sarah later in the afternoon to welcome her aboard and apologized for forgetting her start date. There was a lot of up-front work to do to prepare for the new project. The following week at a staff meeting, Paul officially introduced her as a "beautiful new addition to the team." Sarah could sense a feeling of restraint in the room, almost as if an important client had walked in. She wrote it off to her being the "new guy." Three weeks later, during her thirty-day review, the feeling felt stronger. She wanted to tell Paul about how everyone hushed when she walked into the room. Or how she was often the one selected in the group to make copies or grab donuts on the way in. It felt like more than just the new hire treatment.

On her way home after work, she stopped by a local restaurant to grab some takeout food and found the whole team at the bar having a good time. Frank waved her over. He said, "It is our time to just goof off and not be politically correct. We have been doing this for years." Paul offered to buy Sarah a drink, but she declined. He said, with eyebrows raised, "Don't tell me you can't drink?" and he patted his stomach. Sarah laughed and said she couldn't drink because she was about to drive home.

Six months later, Sarah walked into Paul's office and gave her notice. She wanted to tell him the truth, that she just didn't feel like part of the team, but thought that would be whining and it had no benefit to her at this point. She told him what was easiest, and said she wanted a better work–life balance. Paul was disappointed, but he understood completely. Two months later, Sarah started working for a large multinational engineering firm and has been there for the last ten years.

Although the names have been changed, Sarah's story is based on a true and probably often-repeated example of insider–outsider dynamics. It is obviously complicated by other inclusion and diversity factors (e.g. unconscious bias, micro-inequities, gender representation, etc.).

What is your starting point when it comes to thinking about diversity and inclusion? Do you think that in most companies there is actually something close to a level playing field right now? Do you think fully capable and qualified women, people of color, individuals from under-represented ethnic or cultural groups, LGBT people, and those with disabilities have a full and fair shot to move ahead in today's organizations? Do you even think that, all other things being equal and given the focus on diversity and inclusion, these individuals might actually have an advantage? Or do you think we aren't there yet? Even though there is a lot of sincere good intent, and at least a veneer of inclusive behavior, do you believe there is still a fundamental challenge that is hard to resolve? Do you feel that for a lot of groups, despite all of the good work that has been done, there is still some challenge in creating full inclusion and meritocracy?

Mark remembers very distinctly, in a meeting just after the turn of the millennium, having this exact conversation about the existing challenge to meritocracy. He was sitting with a leadership team discussing their next steps in a diversity and inclusion effort they were sponsoring. A few of the managers hadn't quite bought in. This was not because of bad intentions on their part, but because of their sincere beliefs that they would actually favor a "diverse candidate" when it came down to an employment or promotion decision. It was a bit of a confusing moment, realizing they had a point. In that talent acquisition or promotion situation, they just might make a decision in favor of the nontraditional candidate.

We knew, however, that they were missing the bigger picture. We asked the question, "Do you believe there is a level playing field right now?" They looked a bit shocked and none of them would answer in the affirmative in front of their boss and peers, but their body language seemed to say "yes." To further the conversation, the group talked about how a leader would come to different conclusions based on the assumption about whether the playing field is level right now. We suggested that the promotion decision in the moment might not be the best indicator of whether meritocracy had been achieved. What is the bigger picture here?

Think about sitting in a performance review session talking about who should get the next promotion. You are presented a strongly qualified man and a strongly qualified woman. The performance data indicates both are equally worthy. And it might be, given the history and the lack of diversity at senior levels, that the woman is chosen for the promotion. This scene surely happens sometimes. The issue is not whether a good, objective, and meritocratic decision was made, because in this decision in this moment, meritocracy is alive and well.

The much more important issue is what has been happening over the previous year or two that has allowed candidates to perform at their current level. It is mostly a myth that performance is solely about individual ability and skill. Our performance is dependent upon a lot of factors, including relationships with key parties, support of peers, support of the manager, resonance with clients, being granted necessary authority, and being followed by others, as well as just plain good luck. While the playing field may be level in an individual instance as a decision is being made, we suggest that under the conditions in which employees typically operate, the playing field is far from level. We believe this is due to insider–outsider dynamics.

Insider–outsider dynamics are born at the group level, not at the individual level. We are not talking about individuals excluding other individuals. We are talking about inclusion or exclusion based on group identity. This is about patterns of experience that are a result of group identity, not individuality. There are some key aspects of difference organizations should pay attention to. More info in greater detail on these differences will be discussed in the next chapter. At one level, these various aspects of difference are interesting and can be looked at as holding great potential. Theoretically, a lot of diversity is a good thing and should increase performance as employees bring their different viewpoints and perspectives to complicated tasks. Indeed, it sounds appealing, has some research support, and is surely one of the main objectives of any D&I effort. To get to this place requires understanding the underlying insider–outsider dynamics that make inclusion challenging. These dynamics are attached to most of the key aspects of diversity companies are focused on.

What Are Insider-Outsider Dynamics?

Let's use a simple example to illustrate the concept of insider–outsider dynamics. We wish we could remember which of our colleagues to credit for this effective illustration. Ask yourself or a group of people you happen to be with, "What is life like for left-handed people?" If there are any left-handed people in the room or people who have left-handed family members, they will likely start to reel off a list of the myriad ways left-handed people have to deal with being left-handed. Think about it, especially if you haven't before. Left-handed people have to think about where to sit at a meal or on a plane, to avoid bumping elbows and being perceived as rude. They have to find left-handed equipment such as scissors, baseball gloves, and golf clubs. Their handwriting is perceived as sloppy or as leaning the wrong way (and left-handers frequently have ink stains on the side of their hand). They often look awkward as they try to curve their hands in a way to get a slant to their handwriting that looks like that of a right-hander. Many were even seen as bad in some way for being left-handed, and were encouraged to be right-handed.

Now ask yourself, "What is life like for right-handed people?" It gives you pause, doesn't it? For those of us who are right-handed, it is not something we think about very much, if ever—and this point is one of the distinguishing perspectives that defines insider–outsider dynamics.

What examples of insider–outsider dynamics did you observe in the opening story of Sarah's tenure at the civil engineering firm?

Key Elements That Define Insider and Outsider Group Membership

We can all relate in some way to insider–outsider dynamics because we've all had at least some experience as both insiders and outsiders. Even those of us with many insider group memberships—including the authors, who are white, male, upper middle class, not living with a disability, and in possession of master's degrees—have some outsider group membership. For example, one of us is Jewish and one of us grew up working class. Some of these insider–outsider groups are fixed and global, such as gender. Across the world, men almost uniformly have the insider status based on their gender, and women have outsider group status. Some will change as context changes, such as age. In much of the West older age is associated with a decline and less ability to learn, while in parts of Asia older people are held in great esteem, as wise. As we describe the core insider–outsider dynamics below, think of your own collection of insider and outsider group memberships.

Level of Awareness

When we are in an outsider group, we are much more likely to be aware of the difference, aware of our group membership. Think about how much left-handers know about handedness. Why is this? It is because barriers often emerge that are based on the group membership. If I, as a right-hander, am not aware of those barriers, how can I anticipate or adjust so as to minimize them? When we are in the insider group, "ignorance is bliss." Why would a person need to be aware of a group membership that isn't causing a barrier or a problem?

Ask an LGBT (lesbian, gay, bisexual, or transgender) person who works for a company, "What is it like to be LGBT in this company?" and you will likely have a rich conversation about managing personal identity at work, deciding what to tell coworkers about your life outside of work, and balancing openness against potential risks. Ask a heterosexual person, "What is it like to be heterosexual in this company?" and you will probably get a blank stare. This is not a criticism of heterosexuals. If you are heterosexual, there's no need to think about your identity because it is the norm. On Monday morning, when asked what you did over the weekend, you reply, "My husband (or wife) and I found a great new restaurant in Brooklyn." Does it occur to you that you just came out? Probably not.

If you are white and in a large corporate meeting, do you notice that out of the two hundred people in the room there are only two who appear to be persons of color? Probably not. Does your African American colleague notice? There is a good chance he notices almost immediately. It is most likely your differently abled colleagues are very aware of the accessibility of the building because they need to plan for access with their wheelchairs. Your Indian colleague who works remotely likely notices how few of his comments get acknowledged and built on in team meetings. If you are his white or US-born colleague you probably haven't noticed that, at least as a pattern. Our different levels of awareness have huge implications for forging a path toward greater inclusion.

Different Pattern of Experience

Being an insider or outsider produces a fundamentally different pattern of experience. Insider group membership generally creates a positive pattern of experience. For example, insiders are generally seen as the norm, given the benefit of the doubt, and assumed to deserve the position of leadership they have attained. Nothing bad is likely to happen based on their insider group status. This is a group-level statement: something "bad" can happen to any individual at any time. What we are talking about here is "good" or "bad" happening to us based on our group membership, not our individuality. We are also talking well beyond the random events than can befall any of us. We are talking instead about patterns.

Think about a woman executive. It is possible that on any given day all of the following things could happen:

- On her walk into work, she gets whistled at by a group of men who call her "baby."
- Standing near a desk in the reception area of her office, she is assumed to be a secretary or receptionist by a visitor.
- She attends several meetings at which she is the only woman.
- When calling on a client, she is assumed to be subordinate to the male staff member accompanying her to the meeting.
- She gets feedback from her boss that she is being a little too aggressive and it is causing some of her male peers to not want to collaborate with her.
- She observes four of her male peers setting a date for a golf outing.

Most of these events could happen to a male executive, but it is highly unlikely this would be a pattern of experience for a male executive. These patterns fundamentally shape our experiences and our perceptions. We have seen the prevalence of harassment in the last couple of years as the #MeToo movement, a movement in which women (for the most part) publicly announced their workplace sexual harassment experiences, brought great awareness to the vastly different experiences of men and women. How many men, like us, were shocked and saddened at the numbers of women who tweeted or posted #MeToo on their social media feeds? As insiders, we see these things as unfortunate, isolated instances, occasional annoyances that can be brushed off easily rather than as situations that need to be addressed as conditions that affect the business in a serious way. As outsiders, we see this pattern of experiences as overtly hostile and systemic or, at a minimum, as one that saps our energy and productivity, creating barriers to a successful career.

Willingness to Engage

Outsiders and insiders are often reluctant to engage about their group membership, but for different reasons. Insiders can find it hard to talk about the impact of something they are not even aware of. Also, there can be a sense that there is nothing really worth talking about when it comes to their group identity. Why would I want to talk about what it means to be white, male, or upper middle class? These attributes do not seem like a valuable or relevant conversation starter. In the United States, in particular, there is a value that says we are not supposed to see ourselves as groups. Instead, we are encouraged to see ourselves as fully empowered individuals, in control of our own destiny. We should ignore our group memberships whenever possible, is the implicit message.

For outsiders, the reluctance is mostly based on two things. One is internal: there is a reluctance to acknowledge and focus on barriers outsiders feel they have little control over. To talk about the impact of being LGBT, for example, can be upsetting and demoralizing. The other factor is external, and is at play especially when the conversation is with a member of the insider group: How will the other person react to what I have to say? Will he believe me? Will she think I am talking about her and her behavior, and thus get defensive? Will he try to explain away what I am saying, by saying, "Oh, that's happened to me too, don't worry about it." Will I be perceived as a victim? Is it worth investing the energy in this conversation and would anything be likely to change because of it?

All too often, the conversation is not explored in the beginning because of reluctance on both sides. In Sarah's story, from our earlier example, failing to have the conversation ends up with a separation. At any point before Sarah made her decision to leave, a member of the insider group would have had the most impact if he were attuned to Sarah feeling like an outsider. Sarah really wanted to fit in and succeed at her new firm. She was already visibly different from the group. If she called attention to the atmosphere, it would only make her appear more like an outsider. Once Sarah made the decision to leave, she felt there was no reason to, and most likely had no energy to, open the discussion. Her explanation simply fed into the vicious cycle of preconceived biases, making it harder for the next woman.

Setting Norms Versus Adapting to Norms

Being in an outsider group generally means having to understand and adjust to the insider group's ways of thinking and doing. Much of the experience of left-handers, in terms of their handedness, is about adjusting or adapting to a right-handed world. This norm extends to all, or at least most, group memberships. For example, most women in managerial positions have to adapt to a male-dominated culture. This means adapting to a business culture that is normed around male behavior and preferences. How to compete, how to network, how to distinguish yourself, how to engage others, how to disagree or agree—in most businesses, these are built around male-socialized norms. This doesn't mean women can't succeed but it does mean, all too often, that success is somewhat dependent upon women's ability to adapt and assimilate to the other gender's norms.

Think about the leadership style that is viewed most positively in your office culture. There is a good chance it is normed around male-socialized leadership behavior. There is also a good chance that, culturally, it is US or Western-based. The norm likely is visible, extroverted, and very assertive people. We see a pattern in many companies in which Asians get to the highest technical jobs, but much less often get promoted into leadership and management positions. We think this is at least partially due to the fact many Asians are acculturated into a more subtle and quiet form of leadership, which doesn't fit the leadership profile popular in many Western-based organizations.

Obviously, there are many outsider group members, be they women, LGBT folks, ethnic minorities, etc., who successfully adapt and assimilate. What is the cost of depending upon exceptional individuals to adapt and change much of who they are in order to succeed? What is lost in translation? What is the impact on others, who are quite capable and skilled, but are not able to assimilate quite enough? Are the benefits of diversity in innovation realized when individuals feel like they need to conform to the status quo? Alternatively, can a polycultural environment be as productive as a culture where everyone fits a particular norm?

Implications of Insider–Outsider Dynamics

Progress toward a more level playing field and efforts to create more inclusive organizations are difficult and take time. This is true whether we are speaking of organizational change efforts or about societal change.

Think about how long it took to achieve certain milestones of legal equality in the United States and any number of other countries for any number of groups. Think about how much resistance there was and how much upheaval followed. We believe insider–outsider dynamics are at the heart of this challenge. There is a self-perpetuating cycle at play reinforcing insider–outsider dynamics, making them difficult to shift. Thus, it is hard to achieve change quickly.

The fundamental challenge right from the start is that outsider groups have more information about the dynamics and less power to change them. Insiders have less information and more power. This creates an obvious barrier to change. If there is no "burning platform" for insiders, then why would they do anything? This is why movements for inclusion often start with bold demonstrations of inequality led by outsider groups. The corporate version is often the formation of employee affinity groups. These groups are about finding a way to bring attention to a problem and an opportunity.

The problem with putting out a set of challenges very directly is that it can be risky; it's what some of our colleagues call a "career-limiting move." Outsiders feel reluctant to share their perspectives because they might be perceived as whining and complaining and focusing on the negative, and because these views can create defensiveness among insiders. Insiders almost always have more power in the hierarchy, which only exacerbates the challenge.

To the extent outsiders don't share their true experiences, the less-informed insider perspective rules the day. Insiders' perceptions are reinforced, the perspective doesn't change, behavior doesn't shift, and insider–outsider dynamics continue. This serves to reinforce outsiders' perception that it is too risky or even useless, to honestly and clearly share their perspectives and experiences. They, and we, become stuck.

Often, this leads to adaptation and more assimilation. Some outsiders are better at this than others, and they succeed. Insiders see this as proof that anyone can make it and the playing field is open and level. Are you getting a sense for why this kind of change is hard? We call this the cycle of the status quo.

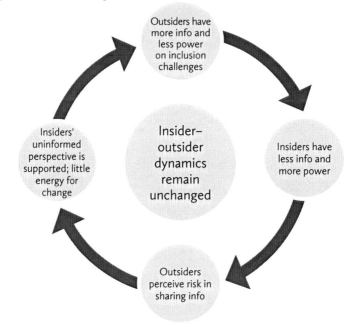

FIGURE 6-1 Cycle of Status Quo

How do we break this cycle and move ahead in a quicker, more powerful way? The good news is that this cycle can be broken at any point.

At steps one and two, for example, what would happen if a change agent inside an organization decided to tap the perspectives of outsider group members? What if the effort was set up in a way that was anonymous enough to reduce the perception of risk? What if this effort was led by an insider, so the power was used not to unintentionally suppress outsiders' perspectives, but instead to fully understand the perspective? Perhaps it would be even more powerful if insiders' perspectives were sought as well. This would allow for comparison of the different information held by both groups. Would it be useful, for example, to get women's perspective on the impact of gender in an organization? We hope you are thinking, "Yes." Would it also be helpful to get men's perspective? We hope you still say, "Yes."

Unfortunately, many organizations ask about the perspectives of outsiders but forget to ask the insiders. In an odd way, this slows the change process. We told you outsiders have more information about what inclusion and exclusion look like in the organization, but it does not mean that insiders know nothing. Everyone's perspective is valuable in a long-term change effort. It is critical to engage both outsiders and insiders when the goal is creating sustainable inclusion. Organizations require all perspectives in order to forge a path forward. It is the gap between what outsiders know and what insiders know that can build the "creative tension," as Peter Senge would say, to move change along.

It is also important, referring to step two, to address the inherent power dynamic. Having a member of the insider group in charge of the change effort can neutralize the power dynamic to some extent and help the organization to get the information that will allow for an effective change strategy. We observe many D&I efforts led by individuals who have visible or important outsider group memberships. Their perspective as outsiders is very important in creating a change strategy—but if they are the only visible change agent, the impact may be diminished because they won't be seen as representing the insider's perspective. We strongly recommend inclusion change efforts include insider group members in visible leadership positions, if not as the head of D&I, then at least as a visible sponsor. This is a strong symbol that tells insiders they shouldn't write off the inclusion effort as intended to make members of the outsider group happier or more satisfied at work. In this insider-involved scenario, a business case can emerge, a burning platform from which to launch real change. Most successful organizations know how to drive change once they have determined it is important to their success and survival.

During the writing of this book's first edition, a presidential election was taking place. One of the major issues was the right of women to choose medical procedures for their own bodies. Historically, political campaign advertisements on this issue featured women. Because the vast majority of politicians making the laws are men, women are the outsider group and men are firmly in the insider position. The advertisements featuring women were somewhat helpful in changing female voting tendencies, however, they did not have a measurable impact on men. One of the New Hampshire gubernatorial candidates realized it would be more powerful if men, the insider group, advocated positions on women's issues. Using this approach, the campaign was able to move the needle not only with women but also with men. The message all of a sudden had a more powerful reach.

Once groundwork is laid, step four must be addressed in a straightforward manner. Insider group members must learn about the difference, and they must have a way to think about it more fully. They need to know about the business impact of exclusion. Because most of them are well intentioned, they need to understand they are not being indicted as bad people. When it comes to this kind of awareness education, we take a strong stance that exclusion or bias is often unintentional, and inclusion needs to be intentional. Most managers intend to be inclusive, so it can be helpful for them to see how their positive intent does not automatically translate to an inclusive outcome.

Ultimately, the most powerful change occurs when both insiders and outsiders are fully engaged. For insiders, this often involves finding our own self-interest. We know this sounds rather self-serving. However, human beings tend to do things that are consistent with their own interests. If I, as an insider, see inclusion as only about helping disadvantaged groups, I may well act out of a moral imperative or a sense of obligation, but my motivation is increased when I also see how I will benefit.

As insiders, we benefit in direct and indirect ways from the inclusion of outsiders. When the Americans with Disabilities Act passed the US Congress in 1991, certainly some people living with disabilities benefited substantially via access to buildings and public spaces. But how many of us not living with a physical disability also benefited when we could more easily ride our bikes with the cut curbs? How many times have you rolled a suitcase up a ramp instead of trying to drag it upstairs? How many times have you used automatic doors when your hands were full? Do we not all benefit when our teams are stronger because we have broader inclusion? Do our decisions improve because of a more en-gaged, diverse group of colleagues?

Research says we think better when we are a part of a diverse group. Find the self-interest of the insider group, proactively notice insider–outsider dynamics, and act to create inclusion without waiting for the outsider group. If we do these three things, we will rapidly accelerate change and diminish the impact of insider–outsider dynamics. Ultimately, don't we all benefit from a more engaged and prosperous society? Doesn't full engagement connect us with a higher set of values, and help us create better organizations and societies?

From the perspective of the outsider group, change can be tricky. The self-interest is obvious, but using oneself as a change agent is challenging. Many outsiders are hesitant to share their experiences and push for change because they are concerned about how insiders will view them; they fear they may be viewed, for example, as being oversensitive or having a "chip on their shoulder." There exists a paradox in which outsiders have more information and less power while insiders have more power and less information, and this condition can really slow change. For outsiders, it is critical to find ways to create greater inclusion. Connecting with other outsiders, forming bonds with supportive insiders, and choosing the most impactful times to speak or act are three important steps outsiders can take. Organizations can facilitate these actions by encouraging forums, such as employee affinity groups, in which outsiders can share their experiences and be supported.

Success at changing the dynamics at step four in the cycle will likely energize inclusion efforts. Outsider groups will feel more empowered; insider groups will be more aware and engaged. This is what will begin to shift the dynamics. If the proper context is created by leadership and change infrastructure is developed, then an organization will have taken an important leap forward in creating sustainable inclusion.

Because insider–outsider dynamics are fundamentally power dynamics, leaders must understand them. We believe these dynamics are at play all of the time, on any aspect of diversity. We all know them because we have all been on both sides. For those leading groups and teams, which is where most work is done in modern organizations, an understanding of these dynamics and the skill to address them are central to team success. As we've shown, diverse teams are high-risk, high-reward propositions. One of the most important factors to getting high performance, or an inclusion dividend, if you will, from a diverse team is the extent to which the leader is intentionally inclusive. At the heart of inclusiveness is the ability to see and shift insider–outsider dynamics. When a leader does this, it is incredibly empowering to team members who are used to fighting upstream to be heard and taken seriously.

Research by the Level Playing Field Institute underscores the importance of addressing insider–outsider dynamics. In an in-depth study of seventeen hundred professionals and managers in US corporations, the institute concluded that "overt and illegal discrimination is no longer the largest threat to recruiting and retaining the 'best and the brightest.'" The research asserts that the largest problem is *unfairness*—defined as "every-day inappropriate behaviors such as stereotyping, public humiliation and promoting based upon personal characteristics"—which causes more than two million professionals and managers who are not white, heterosexual men, to leave their jobs annually.

Other recent research has shown that the development of women in leadership roles in large companies has flattened considerably. In some cases, the trend is going in the wrong direction altogether. A 2018 Grant Thornton Women in US Business study indicates an overall decline, with women holding 24 percent of senior leadership roles globally in 2018 compared with 25 percent in 2017. In that same study, researchers noted that fully 25 percent of global companies had no women at all in senior leadership roles in 2018. There is a common perception that the majority of women leave work due to family reasons. This perception is challenged by a 2018 Indeed.com survey of one thousand women. The top three reasons women gave for leaving a company, in order of priority, were lack of career growth or trajectory, poor management, and insufficient salary growth. For these reasons and more, women who land a job in the tech field leave at a 45 percent greater rate than men.

Again, subtle behaviors—the unconscious bias reflected in insider–outsider dynamics—seem to be at the heart of the ongoing challenge to get more women into senior-level jobs. We say, ignore these dynamics at your peril. If we expect outsider groups to constantly have to "overcome" these dynamics, because everyone faces some challenges, then we are virtually guaranteeing the continued persistence of old patterns and a very slow change process. A lot of progress has been made to increase the development and participation of nontraditional groups in organizations. Addressing insider–outsider dynamics is fundamental to taking the next step forward, and, as is true of much of what we discuss in this book, this requires hands-on leadership development.

Takeaways

- ✓ We are all members of insider and outsider groups.
- ✓ Outsiders have greater information.
- ✓ Insiders have greater power.

✓ Outsiders typically have to adapt to insider norms.

✓ Insiders may have good intentions, but they are innately unaware of outsider issues.

✓ There are communication challenges to inclusion for both insider and outsider groups.

✓ Noncommunication enforces negative insider–outsider dynamics.

✓ Exclusion or bias is often unintentional, and inclusion needs to be intentional.

✓ Sustainable inclusion can only be achieved with greater awareness of group dynamics and skills development.

Discussion Point

Reread the story at the beginning of this chapter and discuss the following.

♦ In which groups is Sarah an outsider? In which groups is she an insider?

♦ What are some of the group dynamics that make Sarah feel more like an outsider?

♦ What are three small things that Paul could have done to make Sarah feel more included?

♦ What are three small things Sarah could have done to manage her situation?

♦ If Sarah were a man, would any piece of the story change? Would anything change if she had graduated from Stanford University?

♦ In your opinion, did anyone in the office, including Sarah, have bad intentions?

7

Dimensions of Difference

There is a paradox, particularly in Western cultures, when it comes to understanding the dynamics of diversity. It is captured in the following unattributed quote, made during a time when racial awareness was changing: "How dare you think of me as black and don't you ever forget that I am."

The power in this statement is the recognition that one of the biggest challenges in treating each person as a unique individual is the fact that our culture is rife with stereotypes. When this person says to not think of her as black she likely means you should not associate her with the numerous largely negative stereotypes of black people and African Americans. When she says not to forget she is black, she likely means she is more than just an individual—much of what shapes her experience is tied directly to her race. This includes how she perceives herself and how others perceive and treat her.

We've heard several colleagues capture this well. Paraphrasing, she says we are all simultaneously 1) unique individuals different from everyone else; 2) human beings mostly like everyone else; and 3) members of any number of groups in which we share something significant. We can look at D&I through any of those three lenses and come to different conclusions. To successfully foster diversity and inclusion, a leader must embrace this paradox: we are both individuals and members of any number of identity groups, and both matter always.

In the United States and, to some extent, the West as a whole, the culture is loaded with messages to treat others as individuals. We grow up with the notion of the rugged individual, the belief that everyone can and should make his own way in the world as a unique and fully empowered individual. We are encouraged to be "color-blind," even though that is almost impossible. Somehow, we think it is rude and inappropriate to notice someone's difference. Yet how can we leverage something that we aren't supposed to even notice? It is confusing, to say the least.

This dynamic is often seen in the context of employee affinity groups. These are groups of employees who join around a specific aspect of identity. They might include a women's network, people of color forum, LGBT group, etc. In these groups, there is an explicit focus on a particular group identity or aspect of difference, and this fact can create a lot of discomfort in the organization. Insider–outsider dynamics are at play in our reactions to affinity groups. Remember, when we are in an "insider" group we tend to not notice difference. The opposite is frequently true when we are in the "outsider" group, in that we notice our difference and have consciously experienced the impact of being a member of our group. The presence of affinity groups, sanctioned and funded by the organization to focus on a particular aspect of diversity, tend to coalesce the resistance to diversity and inclusion. We hear some of the following questions:

- Why are we focusing on how we are different? Aren't our similarities most important?
- Isn't it divisive to focus on our differences? Does this create problems?

- Why should we highlight differences when we are trying to create a unified team? Isn't this exclusive?
- Shouldn't there be a group for white men?

These questions are not bad questions. They are products of our culture, our history, and insider–outsider dynamics and perspectives. They need to be asked and answered. We will do that in this chapter. Take note of your answers now, and see if they have changed by the end of the chapter. Regardless of anyone's answers to these questions, a large and growing number of companies have concluded that they gain great value from focusing explicitly on particular aspects of diversity. This value includes:

- A better and clearer understanding of the patterns of employees' experience based on their group memberships, and thus, identification of key issues and challenges to be addressed.
- A more engaged workforce, as the presence of affinity groups helps a diverse workforce show up more fully and completely at the workplace.
- An opportunity to create networking and mentoring relationships.
- A fuller perspective on company brand and marketing strategies.
- Direct engagement with a segment of the market.

An effective and sustainable diversity and inclusion initiative must include substantial work on key aspects of diversity, in order to gain the value cited above. The dimensions of difference that are top of mind for most organizations, as of the writing of this book, include:

- Ableness
- Culture and ethnicity
- Gender and Gender Identity

- Generational difference (age)
- Race
- Sexual orientation

Other aspects of diversity emerging into corporate focus include:

- Religion
- Socioeconomic class
- Veteran status
- Education

Some speak about "diversity of thought" as an aspect of diversity that should be focused on. We believe diversity of thought is ever present and is affected by the dimensions of diversity listed above. Our thinking patterns and style are affected by our genetics, our socialization, our life experience, and many dimensions of diversity. In many ways, diversity of thought is implicit. We do not believe a diversity and inclusion initiative should have an explicit focus on "diversity of thought" as an aspect of diversity. We do, however, believe that a diversity of backgrounds, styles, and personalities (i.e., a diverse way of seeing and approaching problems) is one of the primary goals of diversity and inclusion initiatives. Focus on diversity of thought, not as an aspect of diversity but as an explicit goal.

Different Types of Difference

The dimensions of diversity highlighted above are not uniform. They vary along the following continuum:

- Visible–invisible
- Born with–learned or acquired
- Permanent–changeable

Visible differences in many ways create the most significant challenges when it comes to inclusion. When a difference is immediately visible, such as race, gender, or age, unconscious biases are tapped in milliseconds. These unconscious biases and perceptions lead to unintended assumptions and behavior. The individual usually has no choice about disclosure of her identity.

Invisible differences create a dilemma: "Should I share my identity or should I keep it hidden?" These differences may include veteran status, disability, sexual orientation, and religion. There is an implicit catch-22: sharing an identity creates a risk that the individual will be seen through the lens of a stereotype, while not sharing an important aspect of identity can mean that an individual isn't fully engaged in his work relationships, potentially impacting productivity. In the post-Vietnam era, many veterans hid their military affiliation because of the war's unpopularity in the United States. After 9/11, it was not uncommon for Muslim Americans to hide their religious affiliations for fear of being perceived as terrorists, or at least terrorist sympathizers.

Differences that are present at birth or are permanent are sometimes seen differently than identities that can or might change over time. For example, at the heart of the battle for LGB equality is the discussion of whether LGB sexual orientation is a choice. In spite of overwhelming evidence that our sexual orientation is a core part of who we are and often set early in life, many hold on to the belief that it is a choice (and should be changed) as justification to restrict the freedoms of LGB individuals.

Some differences are with us always (such as race or ethnicity), and some can change over time. Age is a good example of an identity that will change as we move through life. Our age will mean something different to us as it changes. Religion is another identity that may change over time. Along with age, our ableness is something that is not stable, because it may change with age, accident, or medical conditions. We have the opportunity to be empathetic when our group memberships change.

Key Dimensions of Difference

We are going to focus specifically on each of the six key dimensions of difference. For each dimension we will ask:

- Why is this dimension important in an organizational context?
- What are the key insider–outsider dynamics that create organizational challenges and opportunities?
- How can we create inclusion on the specific aspect of difference?

Ableness

A colleague of ours, Tim, remembers very clearly the first time he encountered a deaf person in a professional setting. The deaf individual was a participant in a long-term development process that included several workshops spread out over a year. As one of the workshop leaders, it was important for Tim to build a rapport with each participant. When Tim observed the deaf participant walk into the room, he noticed her sign language interpreter alongside her. Being well intentioned, Tim immediately went over to greet her and make her feel welcome. As he speaks about his interaction with this woman, Tim recalls how uncomfortable he was and how he kept looking at the interpreter and not at her. The experience was challenging and a bit stressful. It interfered with his ability to connect with her. Tim realized he had to do some work to make himself more comfortable if he was going to be able to help her have the best experience.

To get a sense of why ableness is an important aspect of diversity, notice what we are calling it. The terminology related to disabilities and people living with disabilities is a reflection of the key dynamics at play in organizations. For much of our history, people living with disabilities were seen as "less than," and the language reflects it. "Crippled" and "retarded" are clearly pejorative terms. "Disabled" focuses on the condition and not the person. The language implies a problem. While it is true that many disabilities indeed create challenges, it doesn't mean that the individuals would define themselves by their disability. It also doesn't mean that the disability has any effect at all on the person's work performance. In fact, certain disabilities sharpen other skills and can make a person living with a disability even more effective. In one of the organizations we work with, there was a senior-level leader who is blind. Because he can't see what is happening, his hearing and listening skills have been extensively developed. Most people would agree that effective listening is a critical component to effective leadership. Does this employee's difference make him less capable of doing his job, or does it actually make him more capable?

When we think of disabilities, we tend to think of visible disabilities, for example people in wheelchairs, those who are blind, deaf, or missing limbs, or those who are developmentally challenged. There are many invisible disabilities, including medical conditions (epilepsy), learning impairments (dyslexia), or emotional conditions (posttraumatic stress disorder). The *2017 Disability Statistics Annual Report* noted, "As the U.S. population ages, the percentage of people with disabilities increases. In the U.S. in 2016, less than 1.0% of the under 5 years old population had a disability. For those ages 5–17, the rate was 5.6%. For ages 18–64, the rate was 10.6%. For people ages 65 and older, 35.2 had a disability." This specific dimension of difference grows more significant with age. The opportunity for organizations goes well beyond being accessible for those with visible disabilities.

The main task for organizations is to reduce stereotypes and increase access. The stereotypes about people who are disabled are plentiful. Many people living with disabilities report being seen as less intelligent or generally deficient. For example, people in wheelchairs report being talked down to or having service providers address the person they are with, apparently assuming the disabled person can't make her own decisions. Blind people report having others talk loudly, apparently assuming blindness includes a hearing impairment. The bias, often unconscious and unintentional, assumes that a specific disability affects cognitive functioning in a more general way. Think back to what you learned about people with disabilities when you were young and re-member the insults and phrases that were commonly used. To create an inclusive climate, an organization needs to provide employee develop-ment opportunities that confront and challenge inaccurate stereotypes.

Providing access is a more systemic challenge. The Americans with Disabilities Act of 1991 provided a legal framework within which com-panies need to make reasonable accommodations to provide physical access to disabled people. The Disability and Equality Act of 2010 in the United Kingdom is another piece of legislation that has an employment focus. Organizations that want to distinguish themselves, though, have the opportunity to go well beyond the legal requirement and define access more broadly (i.e., what will it take for the employee to be able to bring his best contribution?). For a company interested in inclusion, the question becomes not just, "What do we need to do to create full access?" It also becomes, "How do we fully access this employee's po-tential contribution?"

Culture

A few years back, we were part of a group of consultants from all around the world. We were studying together, meeting in a different country for a week about every three months. At one of our early sessions, one of the participants was challenging the faculty member who was leading a session. The participant was from Israel. Her questions seemed, to some of the group, to have a skeptical tone that bordered on aggressiveness. Some in the group were getting uncomfortable. She sensed it and became uncomfortable and upset. At that point, one of the African participants got up and asked that the group stand in a circle and sing "Kumbaya" (true story). We love this story because it really illustrates the cultural issues at play. As we deconstructed the event at the time, we found the Israeli participant was engaging in a way normal and appropriate in her culture. The reactions of the rest of us were normal and appropriate to our cultures. The intervention of the African participant was consistent with the way conflict could be managed in his culture. All the attendees were fully engaged and doing the best they knew how. However, it didn't feel that way, and many judgments were being made.

This demonstrates one of the key dynamics of culture: we tend to judge a cultural difference through our own lens, and assign a positive or negative intention to a behavior that seems completely natural to another person. This perception factor provides a huge challenge to leaders in increasingly diverse global companies. It is a big opportunity for those who are able to see the potential that cultural difference brings. In order to get to the opportunity, it is important to understand that the dynamics go beyond a simple difference in style or perspective.

Power, expressed through insider–outsider dynamics, exacerbates cultural difference. In a world where power differences are substantial across nations, regions, and groups, culture is rarely a neutral difference. The difference, which is real, is assigned lesser or greater value based on which group's culture is more powerful or prevalent in any existing context. This creates a substantial challenge for organizations operating in an environment that is increasingly multicultural and global.

To create an environment in which employees from many cultures can be successful, the organization has to be able to ameliorate the dominance of one culture over others. An organization's culture is in its DNA, and it generally reflects the dominant national or regional culture of its founders. This creates a dilemma. To use a Western idiomatic expression, how do we not throw the baby out with the bath water when we look to create inclusion? The historical culture is often at the root of the company's success. In an increasingly diverse context, though, an organization needs to create enough flexibility so employees can be themselves and bring their best contributions. If the preferred leadership style is heavily geared toward a male American model, it will be hard for others to be successful in leadership roles. If some executives lead in a way that is natural for them, they could be seen as deficient or not fitting. If they adapt themselves too much to fit a tight culture, they will not be at their best. To modify an old adage; if you judge a fish by its ability to climb a tree, you will never see its full potential. Addressing this dilemma is essential to the optimal functioning of the organization going forward.

The goal in managing increasing cultural diversity is not that employees become experts in other cultures. There are still some organizations that believe awareness of other cultures' holidays or differing practices (e.g., the way Japanese provide their business cards compared with the way it is done by Germans) is enough. It is simply not sufficient for creating an inclusive relationship, either internally or with clients. Leaders need to understand that cultural differences have an impact on engagement and success, and they need to identify and flag cultural differences that are not being managed well. Leaders need to have multiple tools and methods to engage employees across cultures. They need to run their teams in ways that work for people from different cultures, and they need to be attentive to process and relationship. They need to be flexible in their approach, rather than trying to become cultural experts. Building inclusive skill sets will translate globally. Building a knowledge base of particular cultural nuances will only take you to the next border.

Generational Difference

We live in a time when there are four generations actively engaged in the workplace. Longevity, workplace flexibility, and demographics have created a time of great age diversity. This period is a tremendous opportunity for many organizations to pull from the different perspectives and skills of each group, and apply them to a marketplace that is also very diverse by age. Like every other issue of diversity, generational difference represents potential, but success comes down to creating inclusion. Unfortunately, there are some substantial challenges resulting from the different formative experiences, and thus worldview, of each generation.

Think about your generation, your parent's generation, and your children's or nieces/nephews' generation. Ask yourself what was going on during the formative years of earlier and later generations and how that indelibly affected their worldviews. Did World War II have an impact on the way the silent generation (born 1927–1945) thinks about the role of work and the relationship to an organization? Were baby boomers (born 1946–1964) affected by the monumental shifts in attitudes, laws, and policies that occurred during and just after the US civil rights movements of the 1960s? How did increased global competition, deregulation, and corporate downsizing affect the view of generation X (born 1965–1983) toward organizations and careers? Was gen X impacted by being the first latchkey children (having both parents working outside the home)? Do you think the access of information and social networking have affected how millennials (1983–1995) relate to their coworkers and their employers? How will the Great Recession impact the career choices and spending habits of generation Z (born 1995 to 2015)?

These shifting historical and sociological forces mean that the generations approach work and authority in vastly different ways. This differing approach creates substantial misunderstandings and judgments across generational groups. A typical millennial may think about career development from the perspective of what she can do right now, given her access to limitless information and her huge social network. Millennials need to be engaged and learning at all times. They are not willing to "wait their turn" for the next step up the ladder, as boomers and the silent generation might. What a resource millennials are! Some organizations are taking advantage of their facility with information and networking by creating "reverse mentoring" programs in which millennials are mentoring executives on social media. They also don't necessarily define career development as a vertical promotion, as much as an opportunity to keep learning and doing.

Interestingly, the career development aspirations are different for pre-boomers and boomers as well. For both of these generations money and loyalty were more closely connected to career goals. Organizations able to create maximum flexibility in their definition of career development and keep finding ways to engage each generation will be the most successful. Tapping these groups allows companies to better relate to their current and future customer base. Successfully managing multiple generations can create a huge educational, innovation, and growth inclusion dividend.

Gender Difference

Paul was one of our colleagues. He has a very distinct memory of leading a brainstorming session for a group of managers who were diverse by gender. After the meeting, one of his male colleagues pulled him aside to tell Paul that he noticed Paul was writing down directly what the men said but he was often qualifying or questioning what the women said. Paul had no awareness of this, and his behavior was not intentional. It was an uncomfortable piece of feedback for his well-intentioned self to take in. Pair this story with the not uncommon experience of going into a business meeting with female colleagues and having the man be perceived as the lead.

These stories exemplify what we think is the critical gender-based challenge for most organizations: women need to be taken seriously as leaders, must be treated as such, and deserve environments that value their leadership. As men (and we don't think we are alone here), we were socialized to think of men as the leaders, particularly in realms broader than the household. The messages we received, implicit and explicit, reinforced this socialization. We were simply not socially prepared to see women as senior leaders in business settings. Despite changing social norms, this early socialization persists, unconsciously and often unintentionally. Most women received the same socialization and often co-create an environment that takes men more seriously and values their contributions more.

Very often, gender dynamics in the workplace are viewed as primarily about work–life flexibility and balance, because of women's leadership role in the home and with children. The dynamic of women getting to the middle levels of many organizations and failing to advance much further, a phenomenon known as the glass ceiling, is often attributed to women voluntarily taking a career off-ramp to have and raise children. The data, however, says something else. A lot of research, such as the Catalyst studies we previously mentioned, has been done on why women leave corporations. Work–life flexibility is often on the list, but the top reasons are more often related to the corporate climate and to the difficulty of being taken seriously. It is easier for departing women to simply say they are leaving to "spend more time with the family." When they are leaving a company, they are already disengaged and do not find it valuable to put in the energy to explain the real reasons.

This is not to suggest that work–life balance shouldn't be addressed! We are suggesting this is not an issue for women only. Men also need, and are affected by, the ability to balance their work and personal lives.

This is showing up strikingly with generation X and millennial men. It is an important issue, but not solely a gender issue.

Companies that want to develop a competitive edge need to be aware that:

- In 2017, women made up 47 percent of the US workforce and 40 percent of the global workforce.
- Women are graduating from universities at a higher rate than men.
- Women are projected to be more than 50 percent of the labor force growth in the next decade.
- Women are making progress up the leadership ranks in many companies around the world; this includes not only your organization, but your customers' and stakeholders' organizations.

To build a competitive edge, companies have to be willing to fully engage in the work of creating a more inclusive organization and ferreting out the bias present in talent acquisition, talent management, and the day-to-day climate. It means not only focusing on women and the skills they need to develop, but also focusing on men and the climate they help to create. We believe the majority of male leaders are well intentioned when it comes to gender inclusion. They need help to make sure positive intention translates to an inclusive impact.

Gender is an issue we have been working on for quite a while. This makes sense given that men and women now each represent approximately half of the workforce. Companies understand this situation. In our interviews with Chief Diversity Officers, 75 percent of them identified gender as currently the most important dimension of diversity in their company. Neddy Perez, formerly of Ingersol Rand said, "In every industry I know, the number one focus is around the development of women. That is both on the US and global basis. Women are the number one focus in most corporations. Every company that has a D&I focus will have some kind of initiative around women in place." A continued focus on gender is critical. Since the first edition of this book was published, three important things have happened: 1) many companies have seen gender inclusion hit a plateau, even as women are gaining substantial power in other realms, such as politics; 2) the persistence and hostility of gender bias has become clear for all to see, with the increased visibility of the #MeToo movement; and 3) even more research has shown the significant economic value created when women are well represented, particularly in management ranks, such as large increases in profitability and innovation. Increased efforts are critical for companies that wish to realize the advantage that comes with the full participation of women.

Race

In many ways, race is an artifact and completely irrelevant. In other ways, it is incredibly impactful in defining the boundaries of inclusion and exclusion. First, although there is only one human race, when we talk about race, we are typically talking about skin color. Our skin color is a visible difference, and the most challenging dynamic related to race is the assumptions and stereotypes attached to perceived race, based on skin color. Though the last few years have seen an uptick in overt and hostile racist behavior, we still believe overt racist behavior in organizations is less common than it once was. However, unconscious bias based on race is prevalent. Remember from chapter 5, "Unconscious and Unintentional Bias," the research that demonstrated a well-established and replicated preference for whites? Even when whites report that they are not racially biased, tests demonstrate the opposite.

We believe the biggest challenge in managing the issue of race is reducing unconscious bias, both individually and systemically. We don't
know of many persons of color who have not had significant challenges
based on how they are perceived, particularly by white people. For example, government statistics about racial profiling show that African
Americans and Latinos continue to be targeted as suspects of crime.
The Black Lives Matter movement is a product of the decades of bias
against African Americans by law enforcement. Bias is not ameliorated
by higher socioeconomic status and it does not disappear at the corporate door. Even President Obama noted that he endured bias and
stereotypes in his capacity as a senator and even as president of the
United States. We see the most significant challenges related to race as:

- Unconscious bias embedded into talent acquisition and talent
  management systems, unintentionally advantaging whites and
  creating barriers for people of color.
- Unconscious bias and the impact of stereotypes in which
  people of color are viewed (via stereotypes) as less capable
  generally or less appropriate for key roles (the examples of
  racial bias given in chapter 5 demonstrate how people of color
  continue to suffer from unconscious, unintentional bias—this
  impact goes beyond how whites view people of color; it affects
  the behavior and performance of people of color as well).
- A set of behaviors related to the history of legal remedies and
  affirmative action in which people of color are described as "diverse" and perceived as having received preferential treatment
  or having benefited from racial quotas (This dynamic creates
  an "elephant in the room" around race. Promotions of people of color are sometimes assumed to be due to affirmative
  action, not the skill of the person being promoted. Managers
  may be reluctant to give constructive feedback and may walk

on eggshells around employees of color. They perceive, or are told, that giving critical feedback to people of color might result in a discrimination claim. It often means that honest, clear, and direct feedback isn't given as frequently to people of color as to their white colleagues. This has obvious performance implications and can create a self-fulfilling prophecy.)

In our experience race is the most difficult dimension of diversity to talk about. This is certainly true in the United States, but we find it true in many other parts of the world as well. Our experience is consistent with what we hear from colleagues. Many of us seem to believe it is even inappropriate to acknowledge and talk about racial difference. In the thousands of workshops we have conducted over the past twenty years, we have found that it is common for whites in particular to have received the message that they should be colorblind and not notice race. As we know, this is physiologically impossible for the vast majority of us. However, this pattern of trying to ignore differences is representative of an ongoing reluctance to talk authentically about our racial differences. This hesitancy to deal with race directly can create big problems. When organizations and leaders tiptoe around the topic and become invested in being seen as "color blind," it is difficult to make substantial progress. We have been impressed by the individual leaders we have met in the last few years, since the publication of the first edition, who have stepped up during an increasingly racially polarized time and supported their employees of color. We have seen leaders start dialogues to both create a safe space and create learning opportunities. For example, one leader we know, after a rash of police shootings of unarmed black men, started a dialogue with African American employees. What we particularly admire is her ability to start a difficult conversation and be vulnerable regarding experiences she did not fully understand as a white woman.

As of the writing of this 2019 edition, just three CEOs of the Fortune 500 were black and only twenty-four were women, leaving the largest companies to be led overwhelmingly by white men. Furthermore, 56 percent of these companies had no people of color in the highest-paid executive positions. As the younger population becomes more diverse, the US workforce is experiencing a dramatic shift in demographics. In 1980, the workforce consisted of 18 percent non-white employees. In 2020, that number is expected to be 37 percent. This represents a huge opportunity for courageous leaders willing to have difficult conversations. McKinsey's research, reported in 2015 and 2018, showed that companies in the top quartile of racial and ethnic diversity in their management ranks are 33 to 35 percent more likely to be high performing. This number is significantly higher than the 21 percent figure for companies that are in the top quartile for women in management. Corporations that embrace the change proactively will find themselves ahead of their competition.

Sexual Orientation

The first questions, when considering sexual orientation, are "Why is sexual orientation a workplace issue?" and "Isn't it about what people do behind closed doors?" These questions point directly to a big misconception— that sexual orientation is about people's sexual behaviors. This is a limited view that heterosexuals would never impose upon themselves. Is being heterosexual defined by who you have sex with? We would hope not. We define sexual orientation as much broader and more fundamental. It is about how we are oriented in romantic relationships. The experience of being in love is about much more than sexual behavior. That is true for heterosexuals and it is also true for LGBs.

That brings us to the first part of the question, why is sexual orientation a workplace issue? Again, it is instructive to think about this from a heterosexual perspective. How do heterosexuals come out at work as heterosexual? There are countless ways, including pictures on the desk, random conversations about what went on over the weekend, getting engaged and telling coworkers, getting married and inviting coworkers, introducing a spouse to colleagues, receiving calls from a significant other. We could go on but, needless to say, most heterosexuals come out many times a day at work. Generally, heterosexuals aren't aware of "coming out" as heterosexual because there is no reason to be aware of it; no risk is attached.

There is a value in sharing basic information about ourselves at work. It is how we build relationships, develop trust, and get to know people. When Brian Rogan, the chief risk officer for BNY Mellon, was asked what it means for the company when people do not have to hide their sexual orientation, he said the following: "It makes for happier colleagues. One woman told me about not being able to have a photo of her partner and children on her desk. The first time she took it out was in 2007, even though they had been together for twenty years. We work for the benefit of our families. I just can't imagine not being able to have a photo of my family at work."

This is very important in today's organizations, because teamwork and relationship building are critical to the ability to innovate and be flexible. If LGB people feel it is risky to share basic information about themselves in the same way heterosexuals do, both they and the organization suffer. If you are heterosexual, imagine what it would be like to go to work every day and never let anyone know your orientation. This would mean no mention of a spouse and probably your family. There would be no pictures of loved ones on the desk, no conversations about what you did over the weekend, significant life events, etc. Your spouse couldn't call work. If someone in your family became ill, you'd have to come up with a reason to miss work. How do you think it would affect your productivity, engagement, and loyalty?

With regard to productivity, Cameron Cartmell, partner at Ernst & Young London, said, "Certainly, in a situation where you can be yourself and not have to invest energy into being something else, you will most definitely be more productive."

The next question, regarding what people do behind closed doors, often involves belief systems. Does LGB inclusion somehow put people in an untenable position if their religious view is that it is immoral to be LGB? The correct and easy answer to this question is "No."

Having a particular set of religious beliefs does not entitle one to limit the opportunities of others. Most of us who work in organizations are interacting productively with many people who are different from us in many ways. Our ability to do this is essential to the success of modern organizations. We don't always like or agree with everyone, but we put that aside in the interests of doing work and having a career. No matter what our differences are (e.g., religion, culture, politics, gender, or sexual orientation), we must accept others as equal partners in the work at hand. While couched as a religious issue, we believe this is primarily a societal/political battle being displaced to the workplace. Organizations are well advised to deal directly with any concerns about LGB inclusion, and continue to insist on full inclusion in the pursuit of the organization's goals. A company cannot tell employees what to believe, but it can hold them to clear and inclusive behavioral expectations within the workplace.

A question we hear with more frequency today is, "Why don't people just come out?" This question is a sign of progress. Attitudes toward LGB people have improved markedly over the last three decades. Eighty-six percent of Fortune 500 companies now include sexual orientation in their nondiscrimination clause; this is up from 61 percent in 2002. However, for many LGB people, coming out has been met by rejection and discrimination. Sometimes the discrimination is obvious and sometimes it is subtler. Sometimes it is unconscious and unintentional.

To take this risk in the workplace, the place where we earn our money, seems too great for some. For some LGB people, after living "in the closet" for a long time, coming out is just too difficult. The percentage of LGB people who are out of the closet, though, has increased and will likely continue to increase, and this will make it easier for others.

This increasing visibility provides an opportunity for employers to distinguish themselves from the competition. Caroline Taylor, VP of marketing, communications, and citizenship for IBM UK Ireland, pointed out the benefits in talent acquisition: "If we have a work environment where people are not comfortable about their sexual orientation, we will limit our ability to recruit the true best talent. We will not only fail to hire LGBT candidates, but also straight candidates who value an inclusive workplace." Taylor points out a key attribute to an inclusive policy. The targeted focus is not always on the particular group members. Think of all of the individuals who may be heterosexual but have an LGBT child, sibling, friend, or parent. An inclusive environment, where one can comfortably speak about their LGBT friends and family, has a positive effect even when the employee is not a direct member of the group.

Creating a LGBT inclusive environment involves going beyond the interpersonal level. It is important to equalize HR policies, which are often tilted in favor of heterosexuals. This sort of institutionalized inequality is not only unfair, it is also demoralizing. Equalizing family-related policies so that they include same-sex couples is remarkably simple and straightforward. These policies include spousal insurance benefits but also many other matters, such as parental leave, marital leave, adoption benefits, pensions, family leave, relocation, and even bereavement leave. In the United States and a few other countries, even the benefits was made much easier when marriage equality became the law of the land. By the time you read this book, there will be at least thirty countries that recognize same-sex marriage.

Gender Identity

In this book we are using "LGB" to refer to lesbian, gay and bisexual people, and issues. When making more general references we refer to "LGBT," with the T standing for transgender. It is common to see "LGBT" in connection with corporate inclusion initiatives. We think it is important to note that LGBT incorporates two issues, sexual orientation and gender identity, that are two different issues with different sets of challenges. Sexual orientation refers to how one is oriented in love/romantic relationships. Gender identity refers to how one experiences and expresses gender identity and biological sex. Why do these issues get lumped together? While not the only reason, it is likely because the common stereotypes for gay men and lesbians suggest that each is like or wants to be the other sex, thus lesbians, gays, bisexual, and transgender people are seen as essentially the same. Because of this, sometimes these groups combine efforts and push for equal treatment based on both sexual orientation and gender identity. Progress on LGB inclusion does tend to create progress on gender identity. Many of the companies we work with address sexual orientation and then address gender identity in some way, if only at a policy level. In our writing we are trying to be true that to when we are referring specifically to LGB inclusion versus LGBT inclusion.

Leveraging Difference with
Affinity Networks

More and more organizations sponsor and support groups of like employees, commonly known as affinity groups. These groupings are typically based on traditional aspects of diversity such as gender, race, culture, sexual orientation, disability, and age. Depending on the organization, other groups may be based on differences such as veteran status and religious affiliation. These networks, sometimes called employee resource groups (ERGs), can be a tremendous resource for an organization when used properly.

It is helpful to think about how these groups are typically formed and about the challenges for their maintenance as well as their best use for the organization. Often, affinity networks are formed to give outsider groups a voice and to make the organization aware of the group's perspective. Frequently, a particular group is frustrated by barriers to progress, and both the group and the organization have a desire to reduce those barriers and create inclusion. The objectives are generally twofold: to better communicate the barriers the group faces and to foster networking among the members, so they can better develop their careers.

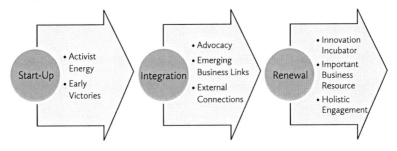

FIGURE 7-1 Affinity Group Phases

Advocacy for inclusion is part of the mission for most affinity groups, particularly at their start. We have found this advocacy typically constitutes the first phase of an affinity group. LGBT networks, for example, usually form because there is a complete lack of visibility of LGBT employees in the organization. Usually there are no role models in senior management, and the LGBT employees who are "out" are often "onlys" or one of a very few who are open. Intentionally or not, the organization's policies and practices do not treat LGBT employees equally. Thus, some advocacy and awareness are needed.

There is an important shift affinity groups must make to integrate themselves more into the business strategies, and our phase model captures these shifts. Ultimately, an affinity group needs to be seen as an important resource for business leaders. However, it should not lose its roots, which are based on the notion of creating a level playing field and ensuring equity and inclusion inside the organization. An affinity group still needs to hold a perspective on the insider–outsider dynamics and push the organization to deal with difficult issues while becoming more integrated into the business by aligning the affinity group goals with the overall organizational goals. Ultimately, no business is going to be effective in engaging a diverse marketplace if it doesn't also create an inclusive environment internally.

When we think of difference we unconsciously think of barriers, problems, and challenges. This can be reframed, however, for there are untapped dividends in diversity. We are unique as individuals, so we all bring our unique perspectives to the table. We are also holders of various dimensions of difference, and our membership in these groups provides commonality and comfort. It is this combination of friction and interlocking gears that, when harnessed properly, can lead to amazing innovation and productivity. Celebrating our dimensions (e.g., through employee resource groups) does not exclude those not part of the group, but rather provides a forum for learning by all.

Takeaways

- ✓ Differences can be visible or invisible.
- ✓ We all have unique perspectives and shared group memberships.
- ✓ Some dimensions of difference are permanent (e.g., race) while others can change over time (e.g., age, ableness).
- ✓ Focusing on the opportunity versus the challenge of difference provides a greater business impact.

Discussion Point

Given the points touched upon in this chapter, discuss the following questions with a colleague.

- Which of your group memberships are you most aware of? Why? Do you tend to be more aware of your "insider" groups or "outsider" groups?
- What challenges might be faced by a woman working in a department or profession traditionally occupied by men?
  - Does she have to do extra work to be seen as credible?
  - What if you change the scenario above to be the only African American in the department?
- Does difference alone provide an advantageous perspective and ability to the organization?
- Does a person working outside of her native culture have to develop a cross-cultural skill set to make her more skilled and effective than her peers who are members of the dominant culture?
- Who gets the most benefit from an Affinity Group? Members of the identified group membership? Other employees in the organization? The organization?
- Which dimensions of difference represent the biggest challenge or opportunity for your organization going forward?

8

Critical Leadership Competencies

Where does inclusion fit as a leadership competency? Is it simply a "nice to have" competency, one that you as a leader should learn something about at some point? For many years, diversity and inclusion work has been perceived as a nice thing to do, the right thing to do, or something a leader has to pay attention to every once in a while. It has not been viewed in the same way as a company's investment in developing a new sales methodology or in technology to increase productivity. In short, diversity and inclusion were not perceived as an investment in the future growth of the company, but rather as an HR check box to mark off. If these efforts were seen as a system-wide investment that would provide a multiple return, more senior executives would have been involved in the business plan to optimize the dividend. Those organizations that had the foresight to see the dividends that inclusion efforts can yield are now leading their competition in employee and customer engagement.

We believe the question today is, "Where *doesn't* inclusion fit as a leadership competency?" Think about the interpersonal side of leadership. If you agree that building a broad base of strong, trusting relationships is important to leadership, then you might also realize inclusion is at the heart of that competency. Building relationships across difference is often more difficult and challenging than forming bonds with those who are like us or with whom we have a lot in common.

In today's increasingly global, increasingly diverse business world, inclusion is central. When US-based companies started to work in parts of Asia, they were immediately faced with the challenge of forging good working relationships. Building relationships with clients and potential clients was more challenging than it had been in the United States and, to some extent, Europe. The challenge started with being able to understand what people were saying. Some of the accents were newer to our ears and simply harder to understand. This interrupted the flow because much of our energy was spent trying to figure out what was being said. Given that many of the people we were speaking with had learned English as a second, third, or fourth language, and it was our first and only language, we did not want to appear to not understand. We thought it would be awkward or not respectful.

The reality was, however, if we didn't attend to the language challenge we would not be successful. We would develop only superficial relationships and would not be able to truly understand the challenges our clients and potential clients were facing. Of course, the accent was a simple linguistic challenge. There were also cultural differences in how to interact, how direct we could be, how to express disagreement. Those were the truly important challenges to building strong relationships. Both East and South Asia are rapidly growing markets. We want a strong presence in these markets, and we can't have it if there is no trust.

Now think about the strategic side of leadership. Growth is more complicated, and it is increasingly occurring in a global context or in the context of an increasingly diverse US domestic marketplace. Apple is an excellent example of a US-based company with an extraordinary global expansion on all fronts. First and foremost, its consumer base reaches 155 countries via iTunes and hardware sales. Apple has quickly become the world's largest purveyor of music (a very culturally based product). In order to maintain high quality and efficient distribution of its devices, Apple has had to create relationships with a diverse set of global suppliers, from manufacturers to retail resellers. Apple expanded its extensive employee-focused D&I approach to its suppliers in 1993, when it established a supplier diversity program. As of 2017, Apple's 116,000 global employees were generating more than US $400,000 in profit each, the largest amount of profit per employee of any company. An environment where employees, vendors, or consumers did not feel welcome would have a real dollar impact.

Earlier in the book we discussed examples of companies that achieved breakthroughs by engaging diverse constituencies more fully and effectively such as Frito-Lay and MTV Networks. This did not happen by accident. Inclusion is now at the core of strategic thinking for many organizations. We recently talked to a company, let's call them WeSure, that was intent on growing its business; it had been focused on one primary market in a region of the United States that was rather homogeneous. WeSure had purchased other businesses in different and much more diverse parts of the country, yet it was reticent to develop a robust diversity and inclusion strategy, feeling that what had worked so far would be good enough.

The leadership team was very homogenous by age, background, race, gender, religion, and culture. They certainly gave lip service to inclusion, but they didn't seem up to the challenge of embracing inclusion as a strategy. They saw inclusion as a nice thing to have, not a core competency. This business-as-usual approach does not work in today's market. WeSure is still struggling today and losing ground quickly to its competition because the status quo rules within the company walls while it withers in the industry.

In most important areas of leadership, the individual leader needs to learn, integrate, and, ultimately, own the concept or goal. To quote Gandhi, leaders have to "be the change they want to see." In no area is this clearer than inclusion. A leader can say all of the right things, but her behavior will dictate the level of inclusion.

Most leaders have great intentions when it comes to inclusion. Why wouldn't a leader want to be inclusive? Inclusion creates greater involvement, engagement, creativity, and productivity. These are all things leaders seek. When inclusion is done well, the results enable growth. As you know, the business case for inclusion is strong. Thus, we meet very few leaders who are consciously exclusive. Pulling through the positive intent to create the desired impact is not easy, however. It requires self-awareness and self-management (emotional intelligence), the courage to challenge oneself, and a capacity to hold multiple realities. And those are just the intrapersonal skills.

Managing inclusion well also requires a set of interpersonal skills, such as the ability to empathize, the capacity to make connections across difference, cross-cultural competence, and an ability to "hang in" during potentially challenging or uncomfortable interactions. Strategic and transformational skills are also important. An inclusive leader goes well beyond shaping his own behavior. It is important to recognize that, while most people want to do the right thing, the organization's culture and processes don't always make it easy. Thus, a leader needs to understand the key levers for behavior and create incentives for inclusive behavior and practice.

Effective inclusive leadership is both a top-down and an inside-out process. An inclusive leader needs to understand and leverage organizational power (top-down), but in order to do this well it is necessary to do the internal, intrapersonal work (inside-out) that will inform the use of organizational power. Don't forget the fundamental insider–outsider dynamics that create an inherent leadership challenge.

Those with the most power to create sustainable inclusion typically have the most insider group identities and the least experience and knowledge of the issues those in the outsider group must deal with. An inclusive leader needs to develop his knowledge and competency sufficiently to overcome this challenge.

What Leaders Must Do

In the first edition of this book, we suggested four areas of competency that must be mastered in order to create sustainable inclusion. The D&I path is a learning journey, even for those who lead the field. Our experience with many leaders over the years suggests there is a fifth area of competency that fosters inclusion: creating an ownership culture. All of these competencies are broad, touching all levels of system from the intrapersonal to the organization's interface with the marketplace. Leaders must also have depth in these competencies in order to create change on such a difficult and loaded topic.

Competency 1: Individual Awareness and Self-Management

Nothing can kill an inclusion change effort more quickly than a well-intentioned leader who says the right things and wants to do the right things but is unaware of how his behavior does or doesn't match his words. This is true for any issue, but with inclusion the effect gets exaggerated since it is the foundation of how welcomed employees feel. A feeling of not being fully included will directly impact productivity, morale and team cohesion. It is likely you already know one of the inherent dilemmas of being a leader: the higher you get, the less you know about the culture of the frontline and day-to-day operations. This is particularly important when it comes to the way you are perceived. As you gain more power and influence, you are likely to get less candid feedback from those around you because they measure the potential impact of your reaction to difficult feedback.

Hierarchy itself creates a strong insider–outsider dynamic, with those at higher levels automatically part of the insider group. Lay over this hierarchical membership the other insider–outsider group memberships found in increasingly diverse organizations. Each of these group identities carries a certain amount of power, and thus has the potential to create distance and add to the challenge of building strong relationships. The more power you have via your insider group memberships, the less honest feedback you are likely to receive. The other side of this dynamic goes in the opposite direction—when you have a high position in the hierarchy, the feedback you give others is viewed as particularly important. As you have likely figured out, the more power you have, the more you are under a microscope: everything you do and say gets multiplied. The feedback and information that you give, and who you engage and how you engage them, are looked at closely. It is critical for leaders to have a heightened awareness in these areas so their behavior will have the desired impact. Following are some specific behaviors that support individual awareness and self-management.

Challenge Your Own Conventional Wisdom

You need to challenge not only your own conventional wisdom, but that of the people most like you. Your perspective as a leader is molded by two things—your own insider and outsider group identities and the group identities of those who are nearest to you. If you are in a leadership role, you likely have a lot of insider group memberships.

We've already discussed how membership in insider groups gives us a particular viewpoint, one that can be a barrier to understanding and creating inclusion. Also, take note of the people who take the largest percentage of your time. It is fairly likely many of those close to you share a lot of your insider group memberships. Can you see how this exacerbates the challenge of creating an inclusive environment?

If you are a leader who wishes to create sustainable inclusion, it is important to explicitly challenge your own perspective and the perspectives of those like you. When an insider group coalesces around a particular viewpoint, it is a powerful thing, and will quickly shut down other perspectives. An example can be derived from the company, WeSure, which was discussed earlier in this chapter. The senior leadership team share many insider group identities. Diversity is not present in this senior management group. When someone approaches management with a proposal to diversify the team for the sake of the company, the group quickly dismisses the idea precisely because these executives have no opposing view to draw upon. Viewing this homogeneity from an outsider group, one would not feel a sense of security in broaching this subject with them. The result is that the status quo is retained. As a leader, you should simultaneously build trust with people different from you and challenge the people closest to you. This is a good formula for building an inclusive culture.

Audit Yourself, Your Relationships, and Your Critical Moments

We are struck by the impact of a simple activity we frequently do with leaders. We ask them to write down the names of four or five of their direct reports. This should be a diverse representation, if possible. We then ask a series of questions about the nature and closeness of their relationships with these individuals: how honest they are with them, if they help them navigate the culture, if they turn to them in critical moments, if they see them as leadership material, etc. The leaders rate these questions on a scale of one to five. They frequently discover patterns they weren't aware of prior to the audit.

We first did this activity in the late 1990s with a financial executive. It was an uncomfortable conversation because as he "audited" his networks, work relationships, and even personal relationships he became aware of how little diversity there was in his circle. While the conversation was uncomfortable, it led him to create a plan of action to more fully engage the one woman and one person of color on his staff. Think about the people you turn to in critical moments and who you know and trust most on your staff and among your colleagues. Think about your mentors, sponsors, and other people you turn to for advice. How diverse is this group? In what ways are you limiting or expanding your own perspective? As in many leadership competencies, awareness is the first step. Awareness, however, is not enough. It is important to use your awareness as a springboard for action.

Build Relationships with People Who Are Different

Who are the people you really know and really listen to in your professional life? Which group identities do they represent? It is a well-established fact that most human beings tend to build the closest relationships with the people who are most like them. The comfort created by similarity greases the wheels of collegial relationships. In the executive coaching we have done over the years, we have asked our clients to examine these close relationships. Almost always, these leaders are most comfortable with, closest to, and thus most influenced by people who are similar to themselves. This is an entirely predictable human dynamic and there is nothing wrong with that human tendency. However, it has negative implications for inclusion because sameness begets sameness. Leaders who do not explicitly and intentionally get out of their comfort zones and make connections with colleagues, peers, and mentors who are different are limiting their own development and possibly their companies' growth.

The substantial research done in connection with the Harvard Implicit Association Test (demonstration test from Project Implicit) shows negative unconscious bias associated with a group can be reduced by repeated exposure to members of that group who are at a peer level or higher. In other words, if you carry an unconscious bias regarding introverts in leadership roles, it is critical to build relationships with high-achieving introverts. Over time, this will reduce your unconscious bias. Doing the work to establish these relationships will have multiple benefits. It will reduce your unconscious bias, expand your knowledge, and model inclusive behavior for others who look to you. Ultimately, you will make better, more informed business decisions.

Competency 2: Embrace the Paradox of Individuality and Group Identity

If you are a leader, it is likely you have many "insider" group memberships. The more insider groups we are part of, the more we fail to see the "groupness." We tend to see our accomplishments, and the accomplishments of those like us, as purely individual achievements. We don't see how our group identities help us, and we can easily miss the way group identities create challenges for others. It is absolutely essential that leaders understand that insider or outsider group membership is sometimes a primary factor in an individual's ability to be successful. The data to support this notion is robust and easily accessible. Research the matter if you prefer, or just look around and notice who occupies key positions of power in your organization and in others. If individual capability was the only or primary factor at work, the only conclusion to come to is that insider groups (i.e., whites, men, heterosexuals, able-bodied people, etc.) are simply more capable and competent. We hope you agree this is not true. Whether we want to believe it or not, group identity is a primary factor in success and achievement.

Let's be clear: we do not believe individual skill and capability is irrelevant! Obviously, very capable people frequently occupy important positions of power and influence. These individuals often have a history of significant accomplishment. Their individual achievements have likely had a lot to do with their success. What is a leader to do? Treat everyone as an individual? Treat everyone as a member of a group? Yes. The answer is to do both. Following are specific behaviors that support embracing the paradox of individuality and group identity.

Notice Patterns by Group Identity

As we mentioned earlier, the first step is awareness. This is particularly important when it comes to inclusion, because our group identities strongly influence what we notice and what we don't. As a leader, you can pull data from your HRIS (human resource information system), organized by group identity. You can conduct interviews and focus groups with representative staff from a variety of groups. You can also just look around. Looking around is free, and it's easy once you start to do it. Who (by group identity) occupies the most critical leadership positions in your company? Who (by group identity) is your most trusted staff? Who (by group identity) do you tend to see when you are interviewing for important positions? In the meetings you run or participate in, who (by group identity) is most vocal? Who (by group identity) gets the most attention? Who (by group identity) has a hard time getting heard by the rest of the group?

Consider Group Identity
When Planning Staff Development

Factor the potential impact of group identity into the support you provide for staff development and mentoring. Outsider group identities often create an additional set of challenges that can make or break success. Over the years, we have heard many stories of highly capable women being promoted into management or leadership positions and facing headwinds having to do with their group identity. Frequently, women experience lack of respect for their authority from men. Male peers or even staff talk down to women in leadership positions, and sometimes attempt to undermine them. It is not difficult to undercut someone who is leading a team, whether the challenger is doing it because of unconscious bias or because he believes the leader doesn't deserve the position and got it due to affirmative action. In research on the reasons women leave companies, two reasons appear near the top of the lists: a hostile environment and not being taken seriously. A leader who wants to create an inclusive environment needs to provide strong support to all staff, and particularly strong and conscious support to members of outsider groups.

Earlier in the book we described the dynamic called "stereotype threat." This dynamic results when there are negative stereotypes about a group and members of that group are unconsciously vulnerable to a fear of confirming that stereotype. Stereotype threat has a negative impact on performance. The threat is "activated" when the stereotype is relevant to a job or position. This has important implications for managers who are grooming members of outsider groups for which there are substantial and historical negative stereotypes, for visible leadership positions, particularly in fields and for positions in which there have been historically low representations of these groups. The theory implies that leaders have to be attentive to building a close coaching and mentoring relationship with these individuals.

Develop Relationships with All of Your Staff

Commit to doing the work to truly get to know each of your staff members as unique individuals. Group identity and unconscious bias often get in the way of truly understanding and knowing a person as an individual. It is easy to make assumptions about others, but it can be hard to really get to know people, their motivations, their capabilities, and their goals. The more different a person is from you, the harder it is to get below the surface. Ultimately, as a leader, that is what you need to do. How else can you create the best conditions for success in a diverse organization? We all naturally and sometimes unconsciously assume that what is important to us, what motivates us, is what motivates others. However, aspects of difference such as culture, gender, and age create very different frames of reference. Understanding group identity is what allows you to treat your staff as full individuals.

Competency 3: Envision and Frame Positive Change

Diversity and inclusion topics sometimes have negative associations. People view them as being about discrimination, quotas, and "political correctness." Sometimes they generate guilt and defensiveness. In many organizations, leaders and managers may view them as a burden, as something they have to do. How ironic! We publicly declare that diversity in a nation, society, culture, or organization is a source of strength and potential. It has the potential to be a huge advantage over more homogeneous societies or organizations.

What is your vision of a truly inclusive organization? What would it look like and feel like to work and lead in such an organization? There is a common visioning activity done in organizations trying to create long-term change. Imagine you are being interviewed by the *Harvard Business Review* because your organization is being held up as an example of a cutting-edge inclusive organization. What would you talk about in the interview? What factors really made the difference? What does it feel like to work in your organization? What did you do to make this happen?

If you, as a leader, can express a clear and compelling future vision you will greatly increase the chance others will get on board to move toward the desired future state. Inclusion is not a zero-sum game. When you create a system more meritocratic and more open to everyone's success, you are not simply dividing up the same pie among more groups. You are making a bigger pie. This is the essence of the inclusion dividend. Following are specific behaviors that support embracing, envisioning, and framing positive change.

Create a Compelling Business Case

In chapter 2, "The Business Case for Inclusion," we laid out a detailed argument for why inclusion is good for business (review it now if you'd like to refresh your memory). As a leader, though, you will need to put the business case into the context and language of your business. It needs to speak to your organization and your customers, and it needs to be connected to your long-term strategy. Beyond the overall corporate business case, develop an additional business case that is specific to your team. Not only will you be more dedicated to inclusion, but your team will be more invested when they can envision how it impacts them locally.

One of our clients is putting the business case for inclusion at the center of its business development strategy. Its research indicates that building effective relationships (not just delivering a contracted-for product or service) is the most significant distinguisher in client satisfaction and retention. The business is global, and the fastest-growing markets are in places geographically and culturally distant from the corporate headquarters. Thus, building relationships across many aspects of difference is critically important to the growth of the business. Inclusiveness is not tangential or "nice to have." It is a business necessity, a critical action. What is your compelling case for action?

Speak to the Impact of Inclusion

It is usually not enough to just create a strong business case. Leadership involves making a personal, tangible connection to an important issue. Leaders are more likely to be engaged when they understand why a change effort is important to them personally, and when they can communicate this to others. What will you personally get from creating a more inclusive organization? What will be required of you to make it happen?

We work with a vice president of IT who articulates this well. When he evolved his team from one that was rather homogenous to one that was increasingly diverse, he saw a marked change in the way work got done. He saw fuller and richer engagement. He saw complex problems being addressed from multiple perspectives. This effort forced him out of his "box," and he learned a lot. However, in order to support this team, he needed to develop his skills. He needed to reach deeper into himself and find different ways to connect with staff. He needed to use his authority differently. He needed to run his meetings differently. Based on what you know now, what is in it for you if you create more inclusion?

Create a Positive Vision of Inclusion

There are probably many examples of inclusion having a positive impact in your business. Encourage others in your organization to view these examples of success as models. If you don't know of any, ask. Look for high-performing, diverse teams. Ask questions about what makes them work well together. Talk about them and hold them up as positive examples. Add one simple question to every internally publicized success story: How did diversity and/or inclusion help with your success? If you can connect these tangible, day-to-day experiences to your compelling vision, you will see change happen quickly.

Competency 4: Foster True Meritocracy

We haven't met a leader who didn't want to have a meritocracy. Why on earth wouldn't you want to have a system that allows for the best talent to thrive and move ahead? Look at the top two or three levels of your company. Are those positions dominated by one or two social identity groups? Are they mostly male? Mostly white? Mostly straight? Mostly US born? From the same or similar colleges? And so on . . .

What is the reason for this? Is it just that people in these groups are more competent and capable than those in other groups? Do you believe that? The answer we have received thus far has been "No." Maybe you think there are perfectly logical explanations for the demographics of your senior leaders. What are some of the reasons that might explain this?

- Women limit their careers when they have children.
- Clients won't accept people from certain groups.
- Change takes time.
- We have limited diversity in our field or geographic area.

There might be some truth to any of these explanations. We think it is highly unlikely those reasons explain the demographic gap fully. In an earlier chapter we discussed the fact that women often cite a hostile environment or not being taken seriously as reasons they leave corporations. In fact, in many companies the turnover rate is higher among outsider groups. Something is amiss.

As we have expressed in this book, the challenge is multilevel and multifaceted. The problem is not primarily individual, intentional bias. As a matter of fact, that whole notion can lead to a lot of wasted effort. If we run around looking for the person(s) who is discriminating, we will waste our time, and little will change. This won't create meritocracy. Creating true meritocracy requires a systemic approach, achieved by looking at what your staff is rewarded for, and looking at your key talent-related processes and changing them so they are better able to support the top performance of diverse groups. Following are behaviors that help foster true meritocracy.

Acknowledge That You Don't Have a Meritocracy

There is no such thing as a perfect meritocracy. We strongly believe this statement. Perfect meritocracy should be thought of as the "pursuit of a more perfect union": it is a directed journey and not a destination. Over the years, we have worked with many high-performing leaders of successful companies in competitive industries such as investment banking and consulting. These high-performing leaders often have a strong belief in meritocracy. They contend that numbers are numbers. If you are a trader, or a consultant, or a banker, there is ultimately a definitive and measurable result. In their minds, when you can measure something clearly and then reward those who have the best numbers, you have achieved meritocracy. It is a great help to have such clear measures of performance that can be reviewed at the end of a performance cycle. The challenge, though, in creating a true meritocracy, is to understand the support required to get those numbers. In most industries, this includes factors such as:

- Networking, which gives access to important relationships, marketing opportunities, etc.
- Informal rapport and relationships, which can grease the wheels for success and provide "the benefit of the doubt."
- Sponsorship, particularly at the senior level, which can increase both trust and visibility.
- Clear feedback, which can help employees make quick, midcourse corrections.
- Peer support, which leads to cooperation and teamwork and allows work to get done more efficiently and effectively.
- Developmental assignments, which create opportunities to develop skills.

All of these factors are important, and they are the primary factors in the management of talent. They help individuals develop and leverage their capabilities. Unfortunately, many of these factors can be and are influenced by bias—unconscious, unintentional bias—which usually gives advantages to members of insider groups and disadvantages to outsider groups. To create a true meritocracy, these factors must be explicitly and intentionally managed in an inclusive way. It won't happen by itself.

Meritocracy is created by clear and intentional leadership. As a leader, you must facilitate open conversation that challenges the notion the organization is already a meritocracy. We find the best way to do this is to acknowledge meritocracy as the goal, speak to the practices in place that support meritocracy, and define the challenges that can interfere with the meritocratic intent.

Take a Critical Look at Your Culture

Look at your culture through a diversity and inclusion lens. An organization's culture is fundamental to its identity. The culture can include formal elements, practices, and processes. Often, the informal parts of the culture are the most important. Think about the following questions, giving thoughtful, nuanced answers to get a good description of your culture.

- What three words most clearly describe your company?
- What are the most important ways to be seen as a leader in your company? In your mind, what does the typical leader in your company look like and act like?
- What are the taboos, the "no-no's"?
- What are the informal ways we build relationships and networks inside the company?
- How would you describe a good "fit" for this company?

Remember, most organizational cultures have their roots in how, when, and by whom the company was formed. Thus, these cultures tend to reflect the needs and preferences of insider groups. Look at your answers to the questions above and consider how the culture is easier or more difficult to navigate for any number of groups, based on age, culture, educational background, gender, national origin, race, religion, social class, or sexual orientation. To create a true meritocracy, a leader needs to change or expand some elements of the culture so it is easier for all groups to be successful. Total culture change is unrealistic, but some adjustments can go a long way in creating sustainable inclusion.

When a client attended one of our "Reducing Unconscious Bias in Performance Management" workshops, he experienced an "aha" moment during one of the exercises. He realized the unwritten "fit" being used to evaluate employees for promotion was totally outdated and not tied to actual success metrics for the company or the industry. Having an intentional conversation regarding what is required of employees to help the company move forward allowed the company to move from unconscious unwritten norms to conscious decisions about future leadership.

Examine Your Talent Acquisition and Talent Management Systems

In addition to changing some of the more informal aspects of the organization's culture, it is also important to reduce unintended bias in formal systems and processes, specifically the talent acquisition and talent management processes. These are the critical processes in the acquisition and development of your human capital. For most organizations, this is the biggest human resources investment. There are many places for unintended bias to impact these processes and interfere with meritocracy. In our "Mitigating Unconscious Bias in Interviewing and Selection" workshop, we give considerable attention to the overall process challenges to inclusion; this includes making sure recruiters are able to have productive critical conversations with hiring managers about potential bias roadblocks.

Competency 5: Create a Culture of Ownership

Throughout this book, we speak about leaders and leadership development. Although "leadership" can be synonymous with people managers, this need not be the case. Anybody within an organization can be a leader of inclusion. If we rely solely on people managers or those who have D&I in their title to develop and sustain an inclusive culture, the effort will fail. It will fail in much the same way that securing your corporate digital data will fail if only those with data security in their title worry about security breaches. Safety in manufacturing plants across the globe would be compromised if employees in the plant, regardless of title or position, failed to see safety as something they had to own.

In the same way, inclusion needs to be something that everyone— from those at the associate level all the way up to CEO—can envision as part of their daily responsibility. In our book *SET for Inclusion*, we write from the perspective of three levels of employees: CEO, middle manager, and associate. Each level has its own inclusion challenges and each employee, when they decide that inclusion is something they can own, finds solutions to those challenges.

One of our clients read the book and reached out to us to reconsider her position. We were in a strategy discussion in which she wanted to roll out inclusive leadership training to her company's top-level leaders. We were strongly encouraging her to create a system-wide plan that touched all of the employees. Because associates did not hire, do performance evaluations, or participate in promotion decisions, she did not see a reason to provide them with this education. As she was reading our book, her company had an incident in which the entire company's servers were infected with a virus because a single employee bypassed security protocols and downloaded files. She said she finally understood why they kept offering different types of leadership-only diversity training but the culture barely budged. Everyone had to own an inclusive culture to make a real change.

Empower Bystanders to Be Owners

Unfortunately, a social psychological phenomenon called the bystander effect can create a barrier to developing a sense of ownership. This effect was explored by psychologists John Darley and Bibb Latané, who became fascinated by the murder of a New York woman in which reportedly more than thirty witnesses did nothing. Darley and Latané assumed the witnesses were all generally good people, but that a bigger phenomenon impacted their lack of action. In several social experiments, they discovered that groups of people tend to diffuse responsibility, meaning they all assumed somebody else would manage the situation.

In an office environment, the bystander effect is far too common. It can involve a situation like a joke that everyone realizes is inappropriate, though no one says anything; everyone expects someone else to say something. It can also be as serious as sexual harassment in the workplace. One of the most discouraging and repeated aspects of the #MeToo revelations is the fact that someone else knew the harassment was happening but did not interrupt it. In team situations, responsibility is often diffused to the most senior person in the room or to the person who is the target of the action. Some common unexpressed thoughts might be: 1) "Well, that was an inappropriate joke about women, but if Mary, the only woman in the group, doesn't say anything, it is really not my place" or 2) "John is the department manager, so it is his responsibility to correct something if it is not right."

Not only does the bystander effect impact social relationships and inclusion in the workplace, it can permeate all types of decisions. Perhaps everyone walks by the oil leak on the shop floor, thinking someone else must be taking care of it. Maybe financial misappropriations in a particular department are obvious to many, but they assume it is not their responsibility to call attention to the matter. In order to create an ownership culture, organizations must draw awareness to the bystander effect and develop practices to interrupt it. It is simply a social phenomenon that can be changed with effort.

Be Ready to Interrupt and Be Interrupted

Part of breaking the bystander effect is empowering everyone to interrupt inappropriate behavior. This empowerment is much harder than it may seem on the surface. Management first needs to be trained on how to receive interruption. Imagine that you just trained all your associate-level employees to not be bystanders when it comes to exclusive behavior. Now, think about the outcome of the following scenario:

Traders are huddled in the conference room before market open for a quick economic update. Doug, the Team Manager, starts to tell a raunchy joke he heard the previous night, when Javier interrupts him to say that the joke is not appropriate office humor. Doug says, "Javier, don't be such an HR wuss. If Selina doesn't have an issue with it, why should you?" The entire team laughs, and Doug finishes his joke.

In one fell swoop, Doug, the manager, erased any inclination that one of the traders may have had to move out of a bystander position. If you want to transition employees from being bystanders to owners, then leaders must be able to receive interruption in a productive manner. In the same way, all employees should be developed on how to interrupt behavior in a manner that is respectful and preserves team relationships.

Leverage Your Insider Status

Although we want to empower everyone to interrupt bad behavior, these interruptions are most effective when made by an insider. We have all seen sitcoms in which the cool high school quarterback stands up for the kid in the out-group and we know how different the interaction feels when it is the outsider standing up for him- or herself. The influence of insiders is not just some sitcom fantasy. In chapter 6, you read about how insiders have more systemic power. When that power is leveraged to champion outsider groups, the impact on the organization is far greater. While it may be difficult to stand up to your foes, it is even harder to stand up to your friends or those with whom you share an affinity.

Break out of bystander mode and take ownership of an inclusive culture, even when it means interrupting someone in your own group who is causing harm. You will have far greater success in changing the culture when you leverage your insider status.

Inclusion is a core and central leadership competency, and we should not envision inclusion competencies as separate from other leadership skill sets. Does inclusion have an impact on team management? Does it come into play with decision-making? Would having a stronger relationship with a client make negotiations a little more stable? Should time-management skills development also include equitably measuring out time spent with a diverse team? The answer to all of these questions is "Yes." D&I development can and should be integrated with every leadership competency. Many of our clients embed our D&I development seamlessly into their core leadership programs. A more robust investment in leadership development provides a fuller payout.

Takeaways

- ✓ Inclusion is a core and central leadership competency.
- ✓ Inclusive, or lack thereof, behaviors impacts all other leadership competencies.
- ✓ Clear connection to the business case will increase inclusive competency adoption.
- ✓ Meritocracy is a continual pursuit with no end point.
- ✓ Everyone, from the CEO to the associate, must own inclusion if the effort is going to succeed.

✓ Like any leadership skill set, inclusion requires practice and constant development.

Discussion Points

As you read at the beginning of this chapter, WeSure is a company with prior success, but is now faced with marketplace challenges due to changing demographics. Examine your company's marketplace situation and discuss the following:

- ◆ Have the demographics of the buyers in your marketplace changed since you first started the company? Do you expect them to change in five to ten years?
- ◆ If so, have your leaders publicly recognized this change and instituted internal change to manage the new marketplace?
- ◆ Do leaders in your organization fully understand the connection between inclusive behavior and company success?
- ◆ Is inclusive leadership development a separate program or integrated into the overall leadership development program? Why?
- ◆ On a scale of 1 (being lowest) to 10 (being highest), how would you rate your overall management team on creating a culture of inclusion? Explain why your rate is not higher or lower.

9

Change Strategies for Creating Inclusion

We have worked with many companies whose approach to diversity and inclusion could be best described as "activity-itis." In these companies the focus seems to be on creating visibility and on activity connected to diversity and inclusion. The assumption is that these activities will increase awareness, and awareness will "leak out" and have tangible, long-lasting impacts. In our experience, while there can be some short-term positive impact from activities such as cross-cultural luncheons, diversity "brown bags," guest speakers, diversity book clubs, and other one-time events, the impact on the long term is minimal and can actually work to undermine inclusion. How could that happen? How could positive, inclusive, and interesting events and activities have a negative impact?

If these one-off diversity events are not connected to a larger strategy and to bigger efforts to create true and sustainable change, the D&I effort may be seen in a cynical light. Employees may begin to see diversity and inclusion as being unconnected to the business. If employees are aware that the company is falling short of its goal to create a level playing field or a meritocracy, and they know there are bigger challenges not being addressed, they may feel cynical or suspicious about the company's intentions. They may eventually believe their employer is using these events as window dressing and is avoiding bigger challenges and opportunities. These kinds of limited diversity events can also be perceived as a way to placate certain groups of employees or more vocal individuals.

We strongly believe inclusion is a long-term change process that must be deeply and directly connected to the business. By this point, we hope we have aptly communicated that creating sustainable inclusion requires a multilevel change strategy that has human, process, and structural components. As we mentioned in previous chapters: 1) the strategy should be based in a solid business case directly connected to the growth and health of the company; 2) multiple levels of systems should be leveraged; 3) senior executives need to be involved and engaged; and 4) both insider and outsider groups need to be involved.

The development of a true strategy is Phase 2 in our Inclusion Initiative Phases (IIP) model. A sustainable long-term inclusion initiative will move through four phases. You may find your organization at any point on this model. This model is only partially linear. Activity in one phase will affect another, and in fact suggest a "recycling."

In these times, there is rarely a true and proper start to an inclusion initiative. Most companies are doing some activities related to inclusion, and the decision to move ahead in a strategic, sustainable way does not happen in a vacuum. Some of the organizations we are familiar with realized the work they were doing on diversity and inclusion wasn't leading anywhere, and they were looking to revamp their initiative, give it legs, and focus so they could realize a return on the investment. As with most large-scale organizational change efforts, this kind of refocusing requires executive involvement immediately. These executives need two things: a rationale for focusing on inclusion and a framework for moving forward. Our IIP model is a framework for moving forward.

The first and second phases are all about developing the rationale for focusing on inclusion.

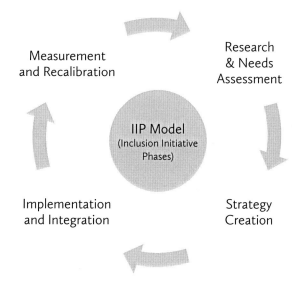

FIGURE 9-1 Inclusion Initiative Phases

These four phases are intended to provide some guidance to your inclusion effort. Each phase describes an important focus area for a successful inclusion initiative. Within each phase are a set of tools and tactics, which we will describe in more detail later in the chapter.

Phase 1: Research and Needs Identification

The primary focus of this phase is building a solid foundation for the initiative. There is a plethora of rationales for inclusion to be found in the corporate literature, including in this book. The need and opportunity for inclusion is practically self-evident in the United States, given rapid demographic changes. This is even more true globally, as many more businesses are experiencing their fastest growth outside the traditional growth markets in the US and Europe.

The ability to work effectively and inclusively across all kinds of difference is now central to profitability in the short and long term. That being said, each organization needs to develop its own rationale, in its own language and in the context that is unique to that organization. Thus, the primary focus of Phase 1 is research. We want to emphasize the cyclical nature of this model; you may find you are entering Phase 1 after a period of activity, with a primary purpose of assessing what you have accomplished and determining a rationale for moving forward in perhaps a more effective way. Phase 1 is also a place to regroup anytime there has been a major change or challenge to the initiative.

The tools for this phase are data-gathering techniques, both internal and external to the organization. They include: employee engagement surveys, HR data, focus groups and interviews, and customer and marketplace data. The data should include key touch points known to be important to the organization's success. A critical success factor of this phase is executive buy-in. Gathering the necessary data will require the consent and perhaps participation of key executives. Establishing executive involvement early in the process increases the probability that a strong business case and strategy will emerge in Phase 2. In fact, the transition from Phase 1 to Phase 2 is anchored in the creation of a strong business case, which is grounded in the research of Phase 1.

Phase 2: Strategy Creation

Any serious organizational initiative has a clear strategy. If inclusion is a serious goal, then there must be a strategy to pursue. Our first question to new clients is almost always, "What is your strategy?" If there is no strategy, we reassess whether Phase 1 was fully accomplished, and we also look at leverage. All too often, great research and data had been collected, only to sit in a folder gathering dust. Or, in some cases, there was a jump to do something in the D&I space because of a legal or other crisis. The jump usually skips both Phase 1 and 2. A lack of strategy indicates that inclusion isn't being taken seriously. When there is a strategy, we can focus our efforts for real effect. When there isn't, we work to help create it.

All good strategies require 1) compelling data; 2) a solid business rationale connected to profitability; and 3) a realistic implementation plan. Assuming the data from Phase 1 is valid and compelling, a strong business case should be ready to emerge. For-profit companies are in business to provide a return to their shareholders; therefore, they need to understand the business case for everything they do. D&I initiatives involve an investment of time and money, time and money that is not being spent elsewhere to grow the business. The business case, however, cannot be defined as finding clear statistical and correlational data that "proves" diversity and inclusion are having a demonstrable impact on the business. It will be hard to find such a level of clear correlation. Fully describing the exact tangible numeric impact of human capital interventions is always difficult, because there are many variables that impact ultimate financial results. Correlating diversity and inclusion with a number can seem like a never-ending endeavor, although we believe it is productive to get as close to this as possible.

Where we urge caution, though, is in using the search for the business case as a way to slow the effort to create inclusion. In some cases, the search for the business case can become a parking lot for those who are uncomfortable or resistant to addressing diversity and inclusion in a forthright manner. We've previously discussed the strong case to be made that inclusion is good for business, and many leaders already understand that there is a demonstrable positive impact from creating an inclusive environment.

The challenge is that many leaders assume their organizations are more inclusive than they actually are. This assumption is due to factors we've discussed earlier in this book, including the fact that much bias is unconscious and unintentional, and that leaders often have many "insider" group memberships that lead them to not see some of the challenges and barriers members of outsider groups face. The business case is not going to convince leaders who assume a meritocracy is already in place to vigorously pursue an inclusion initiative. Thus, the proper use of a business case is to develop a clear focus and direction for an inclusion change effort. It is at the core of strategy creation.

The primary tool used at Phase 2 is a diversity council. This is a group, a temporary team, with the power to create a strategy and possibly oversee its implementation. We will discuss how to best use a diversity council later in the chapter.

Phase 3: Implementation and Integration

If Phases 1 and 2 are done well, then Phase 3 is the exact opposite of "activity-itis." Phase 3 is about directly involving the entire organization with the inclusion initiative in some significant way. This is a high-visibility phase with a lot of work to be accomplished. Diversity and inclusion are challenging topics so there needs to be clear and explicit connection to a larger strategy in order to get the kind of engagement and buy-in needed. Phases 1 and 2 are about getting executive buy-in, but Phase 3 is about the broader kind of buy-in from frontline to mid-level management that will translate to measurable results. There are many tools to be employed in this phase. You have probably already experienced some of them: awareness and skills training, leadership development, employee affinity groups, organizational culture change, and communication.

Phase 3 is, of course, about implementation, but it is also about integration. The critical challenge for any diversity and inclusion initiative is to integrate a D&I mind-set or "lens" into the day-to-day business. If D&I run along as a separate stream from the daily operations and decision-making, the effort will eventually wither. Tools used in this phase must create a practical, hands-on connection to inclusion.

Timing and effectiveness are the most important success factors in Phase 3. What we mean by this is that activities should be "just in time" whenever possible, and they should be done well. We will define "done well" later in the chapter, but suffice it to say there is nothing that undercuts a strong strategy more than poor, low-quality, or insufficient implementation. This period is the high-visibility phase of an inclusion initiative. Visibility brings both risk and opportunity.

Phase 4: Measurement and Recalibration

Phase 1 described a broad baseline of the status quo and identified areas of need, with numerous data points. Phase 2 narrowed the focus to some key drivers. These drivers should have metrics, both qualitative and quantitative. The activity of Phase 3 should begin to have an impact. Phase 4 involves assessing that impact against the strategy. In some ways Phase 4 bleeds right into Phase 1, as the process of measurement is in itself new data gathering. Strategy can and should shift. Activities that bring about the most desired impact should be amplified and those that have little or no impact should be changed or discarded. Keep in mind that the initiative should not be measured based on short-term impact alone. Setting unrealistic goals, such as attaining a certain diversity mix at the management level within one year when there is no turnover at that level, can be self-defeating. Long-term goals should be consistent with your corporate reality. To get a temperature check on long-term goal attainment, review the trends at specific time intervals.

Gathering Internal Company Data

There are a number of ways to determine a baseline for an inclusion initiative. We recommend as broad a survey as possible, incorporating internal measures that are both qualitative and quantitative.

Employee Engagement Surveys

Most large companies survey their employees regularly, taking the pulse of the organization to uncover challenges that need to be addressed. Companies do this because employees' experiences are often correlated with customers' experiences. It is very easy, and highly recommended, that you segment this data by demographic groupings. Measuring the differing opinions, perspectives, and levels of engagement of different groups of employees by gender, race, age, position in the organization, sexual orientation, etc., can provide important insights that might otherwise stay underground. This data also positions inclusion as connected to broader issues of employee engagement, productivity, and other business success indicators.

HR Data

Recruiting and hiring stats, promotion data, performance ratings, and turnover rates are all sources of data that can uncover key challenges and opportunities. It is extremely important to look at this data and uncover patterns because issues will often be invisible at the individual or departmental level. Patterns generally reflect unconscious, unintended bias or reveal biases that are embedded systemically. Seek out alternative sources of HR data. For example, your job board has a plethora of candidate demographic data and can often survey your future talent.

You may have this data already and not be leveraging it.

When using HR data, it is critical not to frame inclusion as a numbers game. Many organizations focus only on the numbers of people in certain groups being hired, developed, promoted, and retained. The numbers are critical in uncovering patterns, discovering root causes, and providing a checkpoint for progress, but if the sole focus is on achieving numbers, the organization won't change and leaders will become cynical, derailing inclusion. There is a paradox here, though. Are the numbers important, and should you pay attention to them? Yes. Over time, numbers should begin to change; if they don't, the strategy isn't working to address underlying issues. Can there be too much focus on numbers? Yes.

In most organizations, leaders are judged and rewarded on the bottom line. Leaders will pursue that bottom-line number relentlessly. If they are given a numerical goal for how many members of different social identity groups should be hired or promoted, they may focus too specifically on that number and miss the opportunity to create broader, more sustainable efforts. In doing so, they may inadvertently undermine the inclusion initiative. Our recommendation is to use hard HR numbers, such as hires and promotions, as touchstones to assess how the inclusion initiative is proceeding. In areas where the numbers are significantly off, do some work with the leaders to get underneath the numbers and figure out what is really transpiring.

There is also qualitative HR data to be used. For example, it is not uncommon to find qualitative and quantitative differences when reviewing the performance appraisals of women compared with those of men. Qualitatively, men's appraisals might contain more specific job-related skill assessments, whereas women's will contain more comments on their interpersonal skills and styles. In other words, the appraisals may reflect the unconscious biases of the appraisers. If you ask individual leaders about this, they will likely answer you at the individual level, and claim they were focusing on the most important and relevant character-istics. However, if the pattern shows up across the organization, a different remedy would be necessary, such as changing the process for how employees are assessed or providing leadership development. An understanding of the data can drive specific strategies to get underneath the data and develop strategies to create change at the systems level.

Exit interview data can also be helpful. These interviews, conducted when an employee leaves the organization, can provide both quantitative and qualitative measures. Be cautious when using the data, though, as it can be heavily skewed. Many employees do not wish to "burn bridges" when they leave an employer. If their reasons for leaving include D&I-related issues, they will likely be reluctant to share that information. Employees who felt substantially disadvantaged may not participate in an exit interview at all. Consider digital exit surveys sent to former employees a week after they have separated from the firm. In today's cultural norm of digital reviews, people are more willing to be candid with an online form than an in-person interview.

One of our colleagues left her employer because the company treated her poorly after the birth of her first child. Despite her extraordinary efforts to successfully balance her work and personal lives, her manager and some of her peers made stereotypical assumptions and comments, letting her know she was no longer valued in the way she had been before her child was born. She eventually resigned. In her exit interview, she explained that she wanted to spend more time with her child. She saw no value in sharing the real reason for her departure. Ironically, the reason she gave fed the assumption that women leave work to spend more time with their families. While sometimes true, this is often not the case, and we suspect this reason is overstated in exit interviews. Thus, be cautious about exit interview data and look instead at the broader demographic trends of who leaves your organization more frequently and more quickly.

Focus Groups and Interviews

Many organizations conduct focus groups to gather information about the experiences of different groups of employees. Focus groups allow a deeper exploration of perspectives and experiences, and can be a critical supplement to other quantitative data about employee experiences. Conducting focus groups of like employees is best because it allows more openness and makes it easier to ascertain patterns that reflect the experiences and perspectives of a particular demographic group. A focus group should concentrate both on broad perceptions of and experiences in the organization and on the specific experiences relating to the particular group identity of each focus group.

Best Practices for Internal Assessment and Data Gathering

In order to fully achieve successful research and assessment, we suggest the following advice.

- Ensure anonymity in the data-gathering process so employees will give candid responses. This is relatively easy to do via anonymous surveys. It is a bit more challenging with focus groups because participants are sharing their opinions openly with other colleagues, and so may not be completely candid. Outside consultants or trusted internal staff should be used to conduct focus groups. Consultants can present the focus group data as an aggregate, which aids in centering on the message and not the messengers.
- Put the quantitative and qualitative data together to tell the most complete story.

- Use quantitative data to help focus the qualitative data gathering. For example, if there is a high turnover of Hispanic employees at the level just below middle manager, a focus group question can be designed to better understand this pattern.

- Remember, data gathering creates expectations, so have a plan of what you will do with the data and how you will respond to the employees who participated. Gathering data and doing nothing with it is worse than never starting the initiative.

- Data should do more than just establish a baseline. Use the data to develop key success indicators for going forward in the inclusion initiative.

External Marketplace and Customer Data

All companies have customers, whether they are other businesses or consumers. The impact of inclusion is as compelling from a customer and marketplace perspective as it is from a workforce perspective. Business research has indicated there is frequently a correlation between the experience of employees and the experiences of customers. We believe it is imperative to incorporate marketplace and customer data into an inclusion initiative. If the data is not included, the initiative will not be taken as seriously by business leaders as it should be. There are several types of marketplace/customer data that can add substantial leverage to an inclusion initiative.

Customer and Client Demographics

Does your company know the demographics of its current customer base? What about those of future clients or the fastest-growing segments? If you think of customers and clients only as individuals you will miss something important about who your customers are and how to best connect to them. The demographic profile of current customers is a piece of data most successful companies thoroughly analyze. However, it is only a start. The customer experience, segmented by key demographics, can yield important insights. We think it is important to ask these two questions:

- How well are you doing with various demographic groups and why?
- Is your competition resonating better with some customer groups than with others?

How much do you know about the way your company's brand is perceived among your customers? Again, it is likely that you and your company have a clear picture of your brand and are actively managing it. Have you thought about your brand through a diversity and inclusion lens? Are you aware of the messages you are sending—some intentional, some not—about the level of inclusiveness of your company and your products? Your brand is communicated in many ways, explicit and intentional as well as subtle and unintentional. Your inclusion brand may have a great deal to do with the level of awareness and skill of your customer- and marketplace-facing staff.

Is your corporate brand being overshadowed by individual executives' personal brands? In 2012, Dan Cathy, president and COO of Chick-fil-A, made his personal opinions against marriage equality public and opened his company up to headline controversy. Eating at Chick-fil-A was seen as a political statement instead of a meal choice. The restaurant chain had to invest considerable time and resources to try to steer its message back to an eating experience, all the while losing an entire customer segment to its competition.

It is obviously important to look forward. The marketplace is

increasingly global, and inclusion is only going to become more critical in the future. Here are some important questions to ask:

- Which demographic groups will create the most growth going
  forward?
- Are you positioned to leverage these trends? If you are in the cosmetic industry and continued to make products solely for white
  women in the United States, you would miss a huge business
  opportunity to provide for the quickly growing non-white population as well as the explosion in cosmetics for men.

Best Practices for Tapping Customer and Marketplace Data

Gathering marketplace data can sometimes feel a little overwhelming
to those not trained in market research. The following points should
make data gathering easier.

- Incorporate a diversity and inclusion lens into your customer
  and marketplace measures.
- Include your customers in your diversity and inclusion events
  whenever possible, and share your best practices with them;
  we have seen strong examples of companies working with
  client organizations on women's development and networking
  events, for example.
- Pull together a cross-disciplinary team of D&I, HR, marketing,
  and analytical staff to create a compelling business case within
  a set time period.
- Think outside the box in terms of the kind of data that can be
  brought into an inclusion initiative.

Tools to Engage and Involve the Whole Organization

The best inclusion change initiatives include both top-down and bottom-up components. While it is essential to get executive involvement early, there is a unique dynamic in inclusion change initiatives. We are referring to insider–outsider dynamics. Remember, members of outsider groups have a much clearer sense of the challenges of inclusion because they experience the negative impacts of dominant groups' biases. Insider groups (usually top executives have a lot of insider group memberships) are usually both slower to see the challenges and less likely to feel a sense of urgency for change. Thus, it is critical to engage everyone.

How and when to engage the organization more broadly is an important decision. We believe a clear strategy should be in place before there is wholesale engagement. Some organizations, for example, make the mistake of rolling out high-profile activities, such as launching affinity groups and conducting large-scale awareness training, before there is a clear strategic intent behind those activities.

Awareness and Skills Training and Development

An inclusion initiative will gain no traction unless there is a shared sense of the challenge as well as the opportunity offered by diversity. Awareness training is an important way to create this shared understanding, and to begin to address the fundamental insider–outsider dynamic that creates very different levels of awareness about the dynamics of inclusion. The impact of training by itself has been rightly criticized. There is evidence that diversity and inclusion awareness training has minimal impact when it is not part of an overall change strategy. Too many organizations roll out "diversity training" as the sole activity in a diversity

210 THE INCLUSION DIVIDEND

effort. This is a mistake, as it raises expectations that some challenging issues will be addressed, and employees are confused when awareness training is the beginning and end of the effort. Training, when implemented in concert with a larger systemic strategy, is one of the most powerful interventions a company can make.

Skill training is sometimes combined with awareness training. If there is a context and an expectation those skills will be applied immediately, then this can be effective. Skill sets around understanding how to better manage one's own unconscious biases and build effective relationships across difference, and ones that address insider–outsider dynamics are among the intra- and inter-personal skill sets. Additional leadership skills development areas include inclusive talent acquisition, performance management, and assessment are most popularly tied together with awareness training. We find it can be effective to blend awareness training with practical skills training. In our Inclusive Leadership development sessions, attendees gain not only a heightened sense of awareness but also a practical action plan. This blend reinforces messages from the awareness training and allows participants to implement a strategy involving the application of those skills. For many of our clients, the action plan is embedded directly into their professional development plan.

Applying inclusion development to a specific workforce context increases awareness and action. For example, our group provides a workshop on reducing unconscious bias in the talent acquisition process and also in performance management. Participants not only raise their awareness of the concept of unconscious bias, but are able to apply this concept to a very real and ordinary part of their daily work lives. They walk out of the workshop with concrete action plans and commitments to creating a more inclusive workplace. Without this application, participants may walk out with "aha" moments but without a clear path that will impact the organization.

Twenty-five years of delivering diversity and inclusion skills and awareness training gives us a strong sense of the best practices that will increase the likelihood of a successful training program. It is important to remember this topic is challenging and even provocative for many. It is important to get it right.

Best Practices for Inclusion Awareness and Skills Development

Typically, the highest monetary and time investment is in awareness and skills leadership development. To best leverage this investment, we suggest the following points.

- **Fits the culture.** Successful inclusion training should be tailored to fit the culture of the organization. Do your employees like to be challenged or do they prefer a subtler approach? Would it be important to have the visible participation of key executives? The training approach should complement and be consistent with other successful training.

- **Done with positive intent, both challenging and supportive.** Participants in inclusion training often enter a bit wary, or even defensive. The topic of diversity and inclusion is a loaded one for many. Some participants may have had a negative experience in previous trainings. It is critical to set a positive tone right from the start. In our experience, most participants in inclusion training are well intentioned. As we've said in earlier chapters, the challenge is less about intent and more about translating that good intent to a positive, inclusive impact.

   On the other hand, it is important to challenge participants. We have seen and heard about programs that completely take the challenge and edge out of the program and end up with an "everyone feels good" experience that doesn't move the needle in terms of inclusion. Insider–outsider dynamics guarantee that a diverse group of participants in a training program will bring very different perspectives. These perspectives, if used effectively, can create a great learning experience. Our basic stance in inclusion awareness training is "You are likely well-intentioned but, given what we know about the brain and human nature, there is a good chance your positive intent does not always translate to an inclusive impact. We believe this is also true at a systems level, including your talent acquisition and talent management processes. We think you want your intent and impact to match, and this program will both challenge and support you to do just that."

- **Includes clear concepts and messages.** An inclusion initiative needs to have a clear focus and direction. It is important to identify some driving concepts and frameworks as well as the key issues to be addressed. This is not only important in crafting strategy; awareness training is a critical communication vehicle, and the organization's fundamental approach and messaging need to be clearly articulated in the training. Participants should not leave awareness training with a fuzzy notion about what diversity and inclusion mean in the company or a vague understanding of how the company intends to achieve its D&I goals. Obviously, we think the concepts and frameworks we discuss in this book are particularly important:

  ❖ A focus on unconscious bias allows for an honest, direct dialogue about how a lack of inclusion can have a powerful and unintended impact on the organization.

  ❖ Insider–outsider dynamics provide a construct for discussing exclusion and power in a way that is relevant to everyone in the organization.

❖ The Level of Systems Framework is a template for the bigger picture of creating the kind of change that leads to sustainable inclusion.

Additional Elements of a Successful Strategy

Awareness training needs to be explicitly connected to the larger change process. Participants need to understand where training fits in the strategy, why they are participating in training, and what will happen next. One tool we have provided clients to help all employees comprehend the encompassing strategy is an infographic (a visual map). This map allows everyone in the organization to see all of the pieces of the puzzle up front. Earlier we compared some D&I efforts to working on a thousand-piece puzzle without the box cover to help you understand what you are putting together, with one random puzzle piece given to you every couple of months. This is what D&I can feel like to those not aware of the entire strategy. They attend an awareness workshop one month, and then six months later they attend an event sponsored by an employee resource group. Every year they get three or four pieces of the puzzle. Knowing the entire strategy up front allows all employees to more effectively integrate D&I into everyday decisions.

To draw out this metaphor, a constant flow of pieces will help increase engagement. Training should be ongoing, not a one-time event. Other methods include learning sustainment activities that go beyond traditional classroom workshops, such as newsletters or internal blogs, occasional awareness events (i.e., lectures, outsider speakers, lunchtime learning events), webinars, and web-based learning tools.

There should be additional development focused on leaders. Inclusion is fundamentally a leadership challenge, and leaders should be supported to meet the challenge. Development should be targeted, be connected to a broader strategic plan, and include accountability. Our clients do this in a number of different ways.

In some organizations, leaders are given specific, just-in-time training to reduce the impact of unconscious, unintended bias in the performance appraisal process. Training is connected to a strategy to make the appraisal process more effective and inclusive. The strategy is based on data showing some possible unintended inequities in the process.

In another organization, leaders of client-facing teams are being asked to work with their teams to increase the effectiveness and inclusiveness of their client relationships. Work is anchored in data that shows the importance of relationship building in client retention and development.

Other clients we have partnered with have specific numerical goals over several years to increase recruitment of diverse groups, reduce turnover, and increase promotions. Leadership development activities are essential to support leaders in pursuing these goals skillfully and in creating a more inclusive overall climate. Otherwise, the inclusion effort can become a "numbers game," increasing suspicion, decreasing morale and performance, and eroding the organization in the long run.

Affinity Networks

Successful affinity groups will not be exclusive. While there must be an opportunity for frank dialogue, and support and mentoring of group members is the focus, all members of the organization need to be able to be involved. LGBT groups are particularly effective in this area because they have to be visible. As noted in chapter 7, "Dimensions of Difference," there are visible (those easily seen) and invisible (those that need to be self-identified) differences. Sexual orientation is an invisible difference that requires self-identification. Many LGBT employees are in the closet and are unsure about coming out, so the groups need visible heterosexual allies. All affinity groups can and should find ways to involve the whole organization. There are many ways to achieve this level of involvement:

- Educational events sponsored by the affinity group.
- Activities that involve multiple affinity groups.
- Marketplace forums highlighting key demographic information.
- General networking events.
- Mentoring and sponsorship programs that involve senior leaders supporting affinity group members.
- "Reverse" mentoring where affinity group members are coaching executives.
- Community-based events with partnered business leaders and affinity group members.

Best Practices for Affinity Groups

In addition to the best practices related to increasing affinity groups' involvement with the rest of the organization, we have some advice for effective affinity group programs:

- **From the start, the affinity groups should be chartered** to support members of the network and the organization. Ensure there is a clear charter and a set of broad objectives that speak to both of these concerns.
- **Involve business leaders.** Visible and active sponsorship will dispel concerns that the affinity groups are non-inclusive and divisive. Each affinity group should have at least one executive sponsor. It is important that these sponsors have an active role

in shaping a strategic plan and setting objectives that position the group effectively.

- **Affinity groups should be immediately linked to the business in some tangible way.** A visible executive sponsor helps. There needs to be a more tangible connection that might include: increasing the inclusiveness of the climate, improving the talent acquisition and talent management practices, and/ or helping the organization more fully engage the marketplace, customers, and communities.

- **Open affinity groups to all staff.** Sponsor activities involving others. Consider opening the membership rolls to everyone (specifically allies).

Tools to Create Systemic Process Change

Systemic process change is one of the hardest to accomplish because it requires awareness at the other two primary levels (individual and group). The following tools will provide a step up to achieving this change.

Meritocracy Review

A central goal of any inclusion initiative should be to create a living, breathing meritocracy. This should be a substantial focus of Phase 3. It involves looking at all of the organization's people-related processes, particularly those involving the acquisition and development of talent. A meritocracy, which is the goal of most organizations, is brought to life by two things: 1) leaders who are committed to conscious and intentional creation of an environment that brings out the best in all groups of employees; 2) structures and processes that support inclusion and minimize the impact of unconscious, unintentional bias.

These processes are at the core of the company's management of its biggest investment: its people. If these processes aren't fully inclusive, it will be impossible to achieve an inclusive organization. We believe a meritocracy review is an essential step in an inclusion change process. The heart of a meritocracy review involves evaluating the talent acquisition and talent management processes to 1) challenge embedded assumptions about qualifications, needed skills, critical competencies, success indicators, etc. that are not the best predictors of success; 2) look for unconscious, unintentional bias anywhere in these processes; and 3) identify changes that minimize bias and increase objectivity, and thus enhance meritocracy. Earlier in the book, you may recall we call these changes "System 2 moments" or steps in the process that help to challenge assumptions, temporarily slow down decision-making, or expand the perspectives being provided.

A meritocracy review is fairly simple but requires committing the time and energy of the right team members, including the HR specialists who design and "own" the talent acquisition and talent management processes, business leaders who are the customers and end users of these processes, and D&I experts.

Typical process changes resulting from a meritocracy review might include:

- Blind screening of résumés and other techniques that reduce unintended bias on the front end of the talent acquisition process.
- Structured behavioral interviewing built around proven job competencies.
- Multisource input for all talent acquisition and talent management decisions, as a requirement.
- 9-box grid (an individual assessment tool) or similar processes to assess talent, that allows for simultaneous comparison of talent by a leadership team 360-degree performance feedback.

- "System 2 moments" inserted at key points during talent acquisition and talent management processes, such as:
  - ❖ Hiring decisions for key positions or certain levels made by a diverse panel with anonymous input.
  - ❖ Rigorous talent reviews conducted by a diverse group of leaders, with an explicit diversity and inclusion lens.

These process changes do not guarantee meritocracy, but they certainly help in the pursuit of a more genuine meritocracy. Leverage these suggestions as tools that can help you achieve the goal, but don't count on them as sure fixes in and of themselves. In 2018, anti-bias technology emerged in talent acquisition. Be careful not to rely solely on technology to remove biases for two important reasons: 1) in the end, humans make the hiring decision; and 2) technology is coded by humans with biases, and they can embed their biases into the system. In the same vein, multisource input doesn't necessarily create more objective decisions: insider–outsider dynamics may create reluctance in members of outsider groups to voice their full perspective if they feel they won't be seen as credible or as "team players." HR staff and leaders have to be developed to understand insider–outsider dynamics, to know which questions to ask, to be willing to discover their own biases, and to make it safe for others to raise tough issues and to make change stick.

Best Practices for Implementing a Meritocracy Review

At the beginning of the book we discussed how the great majority of executives believe a meritocracy already exists within the organization. Therefore, implementing a review to determine the level of meritocracy may receive some push-back. There are a number of resources and methods to accomplish this review effectively. Below are a few tips.

- Involve business leaders and HR executives.
- Use multiple sources of data.
- Do not seek to lay blame.
- Use affinity groups as a resource.

Organizational Culture Shaping

True culture change is an ambitious goal that can take years or decades. We are not opposed to culture change, but we think much can be done to increase inclusion short of total culture change. We suggest identifying elements of the culture that are core to inclusion and working to change them in the desired direction. Because this should be a values-based change process, we suggest it involve the most senior executive levels and be guided by internal and external experts.

One company we worked with recently revamped its core values to integrate inclusion into them. This process was taken very seriously, with top executives involved extensively for more than a year. It was just the beginning. The values are being rolled out in multiple forums, integrated into key training and development activities, and included in performance appraisals. The best way to conduct a culture-shaping process for an inclusion initiative is to make it part of a larger effort to evolve the company's values and culture. In this way, inclusion is explicitly integrated.

An inclusion initiative can, in fact, add some perspective to a culture-shaping process because it provides an opportunity to shape the culture from the perspective of insider and outsider groups. This is often missed in larger culture change or values development initiatives. A well-done inclusion initiative will have a set of organizational values and behaviors at its core, and these can enhance and deepen the organizational values. The organization's values can both inform and be informed by the inclusion initiative.

Methods: The Infrastructure for Change

We have already described the need for a robust change effort led from the top, supported by a strong business case, a strategic plan, and smart use of a number of tools. If these are the bricks, there also needs to be some mortar. A robust inclusion initiative needs infrastructure, some of which will be temporary. There are four primary pieces of infrastructure required for a robust inclusion initiative: a diversity council, a Diversity and Inclusion Department, an HR D&I integration task force, and an inclusion marketing function.

Diversity Council

A diversity council can be an effective tool for creating a strategy (Phase 2) and jump-starting or overseeing implementation (Phase 3). An effective council will have the involvement or direct sponsorship of the CEO and its members will include leaders with broad decision-making authority. It should be given a clear mandate and goal. We have seen councils fail when they are created without a clear mandate, budget, or decision-making authority. Without a high level of support, a council can quickly join the game of "activity-itis." The business leaders should "own" the council, not Human Resources or the Diversity and Inclusion function. Those functions are critical, however, for bringing an important perspective and expertise, and they should guide and facilitate the council.

A diversity council's primary role is to act as a bridge between the business case for action and the strategy's implementation. It has several key roles:

Strategy Development

Strategy development is the primary job of the diversity council. The council needs to take the Phase 1 data, narrow in on the most import-ant challenges, and create a strategy to address them. A good strategy will have both short- and long-term elements. It is important to have a strong short-term strategy that creates some early wins and a good vibe for the initiative.

Change Management

In creating the strategy and planning for the implementation, the council needs to anticipate the support for and resistance to the strategy. These factors have to be directly addressed in the strategy and implementation. As we discussed earlier in the book, you should use other successful organizational change efforts as a guide. Don't forget the unique dynamics that go along with D&I initiatives. These insider–outsider dynamics create particular challenges. The change management role of the council needs to anticipate and prepare for these dynamics as the strategy is implemented.

Communication

The council needs to ensure that the intent of the inclusion initiative is clear, and that there is a focused and coherent message. The topics of diversity and inclusion can be provocative, and misinterpretations can be rife. The communication strategy must be straightforward, without

D&I-specific jargon. It should include multiple media and should connect the business case to the implementation tools and activities.

Best Practices for Diversity Councils

We have unfortunately seen too many diversity councils fail to accomplish their original goal of engaging leadership and staff to create a more inclusive culture. Below are a few best practices to help ensure the council is most effective.

- Ensure sponsorship and involvement of top executives; more critically, ensure the involvement of leaders of core revenue-generating functions.
- Include a mix of insider and outsider group members so multiple perspectives are represented on the council; get the most out of diverse representation with a process that will create a safe team environment on the council, allowing for frank dialogue.
- Provide both authority and accountability to the council so members are invested in the outcome and the council is taken seriously in the organization.
- Utilize a clear set of concepts and frameworks to guide the strategy development; there are a number of ways to approach inclusion work (e.g., levels of systems focus, insider–outsider dynamics, unconscious bias). Pick ones that will resonate in your organization.
- Utilize external expertise to both help the council work together effectively and choose the best concepts and frameworks; a diversity council has a challenging task, and deep external expertise will be needed.

Diversity and Inclusion Department

The D&I Department has the primary role of internal change agent for inclusion. This is a visible and risky role, and thus the D&I function must be positioned for maximum impact. To facilitate this, D&I should not be put under the HR function but instead positioned as a partner with HR. HR has a specific and critical role in an inclusion initiative—to integrate an inclusion lens into all talent acquisition and talent management processes. The D&I function can too easily get lost in the HR function, both practically and politically. This is a mistake because HR is a permanent and ongoing function while D&I is in the role of change agent, and at least part of its function will be temporary and dependent upon the phase of the initiative. Additionally, D&I should be interfacing with many other parts of the organization, such as Marketing, Public Relations, Sales Department, and the Operating Committee. D&I has an internal (employees) and an external (the marketplace) component. Many organizations have created a chief diversity officer (CDO) position to elevate the D&I function and position it at the executive level. The CDOs we have seen reporting to an operational position like CEO or COO often have a much higher budget than those reporting into an HR function. They also tend to be more closely connected to market results.

Chief Diversity Officer is an increasingly common title, but more organizations focusing on the inclusion aspect are renaming the title Chief Inclusion Officer. Whatever you call the position, make sure the person you tap has the business experience and presence to engage your executive team. Some organizations rotate business line executives in this position as a one- to two-year assignment. We like this model because it constantly brings in new viewpoints. It is critical the executive has access to expert D&I guidance via an external consultant and support from an expert internal team. Companies would never think of putting someone in a chief financial officer role without the help of the internal finance and accounting team in addition to the external auditing team. They should be as careful with the CDO role.

The person who is hired into the diversity executive role is critical to the way the initiative is understood and supported. We have seen large companies choose as chief diversity officer individuals who don't have the seniority or business knowledge requisite for an executive position. This is a death knell to an inclusion initiative. D&I requires a person who has experience creating successful systemic change initiatives and managing challenging conversations, and who can be a public-facing company representative to the market. CDOs are commonly asked to sit on panels and are often interviewed on behalf of the company.

Considering only individuals with mostly outsider group memberships for the most senior diversity position is a common pitfall. It can be very powerful to put an individual with multiple insider group memberships in the top diversity job, as long as the person is committed to the work and has access to other expertise. Such an executive will likely have the kind of credibility that pushes the inclusion initiative forward.

HR D&I Integration Task Force

HR should not oversee the D&I work, but it should be intimately involved in the way inclusion is integrated into day-to-day management and leadership behavior in the organization. Every function of HR has a role. The recruiting function can focus on creating more diverse, inclusive pipelines of potential employees. Recruiters can also change the interviewing and selection processes to make sure unconscious bias is minimized. Compensation and benefits specialists can review the financial and nonfinancial compensation to ensure it meets the needs of an increasingly diverse workforce. The compensation function can identify and address potential systemic bias in the compensation system. The talent management function can work to ensure the key development processes are inclusive.

Because of the powerful impact of networking and relationships, talented employees can be overlooked, not mentored or sponsored, and not included on "high-potential" lists or in succession plans. The training and development function needs to ensure inclusion is integrated into employee development programs beyond inclusion development. Finally, HR generalists have perhaps the most critical role because they are frequently the day-to-day advisors and coaches to leaders who are making decisions about people on a daily basis. The full integration of inclusion is largely dependent upon the extent to which HR generalists are supported and developed to bring an inclusion lens to their work.

In order to do this work in a meaningful way, the HR D&I integration task force should include business leaders (the clients of HR) and D&I experts to make sure that the critical questions are asked and the changes will stick.

Inclusion Marketing Function

"Multicultural marketing" is becoming a more common organizational function in large companies. Typically, this function looks at positioning the company for success in particular niche markets. For example, a company may set up a function to concentrate on the LGBT market segment. Avoid the trap, though, of seeing diverse markets as only niche markets, to be appealed to in certain specific ways. This would be parallel to hiring a sales force to match the customers; that is, to have Indian salespeople call on Indian customers. While this approach can be helpful, it is also limiting. We believe a state-of-the-art inclusion marketing function will look at the broader challenge of creating inclusion across the whole product line, actually integrating an inclusion lens into the entire marketing function. We believe this allows the possibility of breakthroughs in product development and marketing. This approach assumes inclusion is a part of all marketing decisions.

Making It Stick

An inclusion initiative is quite a bit like any large organizational change process. It requires compelling data, a strong business case, a solid strategy, and effective engagement of all stakeholders. However, it also needs two other pieces: accountability and leadership. For anything to shift meaningfully, leaders have to be held accountable for creating change. We strongly recommend including some of the key success metrics of the strategy on the performance goals of leaders initially, and on the goals of all managers, supervisors, and individual contributors eventually.

Some organizations create "diversity scorecards" and use them to evaluate leaders' performance. We strongly recommend this approach, with two caveats. First, it is essential that these measures are not primarily promotion and representation numbers, particularly as short-term goals. This would only fuel the notion that inclusion is more about numbers. Second, leaders should be evaluated based on what they can reasonably control or influence. We think they can be fairly evaluated on some quantitative and qualitative measures such as increasing the diversity of hiring pools, reducing unwanted turnover rates of "outsider" groups, and development activities they participate in and/or lead.

The leadership required is substantial. Beyond what we have already described, leaders will need to be prepared to manage reactions to the inclusion work. Insider–outsider dynamics predict certain reactions. Outsider groups will be skeptical the change is real, as they are used to lip service and are aware the playing field is not level in many subtle ways. Insider groups will explicitly or, more often, implicitly, see the change as creating a nonlevel playing field in the other direction. Leaders need to understand this, plan for it, and engage it. Remember, resistance to change is a good thing! It often means the change is real; otherwise, there would be no need for resistance. Leaders' behavior in the face of resistance will predict the success of the initiative.

Like everything else you do as leaders, successful change always comes down to commitment, authenticity, engagement, and persistence.

Takeaways

- ✓ D&I needs a short- and a long-term strategy.
- ✓ The foundation of a D&I initiative is a research and needs analysis.
- ✓ D&I strategy connected to a clear business case is most successful at employee engagement.
- ✓ Simply scheduling a calendar of events is not a strategy.
- ✓ Like any strategy, D&I needs metrics and periodic review.
- ✓ There are many tools to reach D&I goals.
- ✓ All tools, such as employee resource groups, need to be aligned with a business case.
- ✓ Providing all employees with a visualization of the compelling overall strategy will help with adoption and achievement of the plan.
- ✓ Investing in D&I is just that, an investment, and should be expected to deliver tangible dividends.
- ✓ Dedicated D&I staff, such as a chief diversity officer (CDO), will help ensure that proper attention is given to achieving established goals.

Discussion Point

Randy received an event alert reminding him about the celebration of cross-cultural cooking being sponsored by the corporate HR team to promote inclusion. The event sounded fun, and free food was always a draw for him. He'd enjoyed the music event put on by the Asian employee resource group last month. The company had hired a HR diversity coordinator, who has been great at creating a calendar of engaging events.

Randy is a director of marketing for a sixty-thousand-employee company focused on children's retail. His department has been trying to tap into the rapidly growing Latino segment. The company has not had success with previous campaigns, but he mostly blames the buyer team for not finding the right products. Marketing has hired external focus groups and done extensive market research to really fine-tune the communication campaign. Randy thought going to the cross-cultural event would help him get his mind off work for a while. "Hope they have something Italian," he found himself thinking.

- ♦ What do you think Randy's thoughts are about his company's D&I initiative?
- ♦ From the short description of Randy's job and current challenge, how do you think D&I could help?
- ♦ Do you believe his company has formulated a D&I strategy? Developed a business case?
- ♦ Where could D&I produce a tangible dividend?

Conclusion

At the beginning of this book we introduced you to Asha. She, like most leaders, had the best intent to move her company and herself forward. All the while, she really had not thought about all of this "diversity and inclusion HR stuff" as a way to help her reach both those goals. She came to understand that, much like building her 401K, D&I was all about the long-term strategy, and there was a lot to learn. We wanted to get you into the investment frame of mind from the start. This is what many psychologists would call priming. We wanted you to digest this book and its concepts with an eye toward how investing your time and resources in building an inclusive environment would pay dividends over time.

Providing historical background to D&I gave you an idea of where we, as a country and as employers, started as well as how far we still need to go. Because the old view of D&I was steeped in legal compliance and litigation it was important for you to know some of the legislation that helped frame this perception. Just as important is knowing how changing demographics and traditional exclusion had created barriers for growth for those organizations not prepared for change. On the other hand, these same two aspects provided many more opportunities for companies to take an inclusive approach and leap frog their competition.

Along the way you were introduced to Francis, who discovered that his company's approach to talent management very much mirrored its approach to clients. If talent acquisition and talent management were transactional, for the most part, client relationships were transactional as well. Both talent and clients were easily separated from their relationship with the organization. Thus, the business case for inclusion was expanded from the traditional employee focus to an external focus on the community and marketplace.

After the conversation with Francis, you got a sneak peek at a typical busy day in the life of a leader by looking over Kim's shoulder. Kim's day was probably not unlike yours or those of leaders you know. It was a regular day like many others. We chose to share Kim's regular day with you to explain how the concepts of diversity and inclusion live in our everyday lives and decisions. D&I cannot and should not be an event you attended or box you checked: it lives and breathes within our work and after-work life. It takes an intentional leader to develop a process that integrates these concepts within, not separate from, our overall decision-making philosophy.

If leaders simply look at the individual level, they miss a huge opportunity to instill change. We spoke of four distinct levels that all influence one another and share common space. When individual development is coupled with the group/team, systemic, and marketplace levels, an organization can achieve a much higher return. To return to our overarching example: Asha could not simply put her money into mutual funds and magically expect a great return. Her financial strategy involved understanding the market, her company, her changing individual goals and compensation, and the mutual fund system itself. Rarely does a strategy of any kind succeed without a holistic viewpoint. D&I is no different.

Even the creation of a strategy can be skewed if we do not first take the time to understand our own biases and how they may be influencing any one of these levels. You read about how unconscious bias was impacting both Raul and Doris, what they consciously did to mitigate it, and the result. Many studies have been published in the realm of unconscious bias, with the aim of understanding why our behaviors may have unintended impacts when the original intent was good. This area of study hopefully allows us to move the conversation forward without the guilt or defensiveness that often accompanies D&I exploration.

Once we have been introduced to the concept of unconscious bias, the conversation can take another step forward by discussing insider–outsider groups. Sarah's story was a prime example of unintended results emanating from insider–outsider behavior. When conversation is absent, the unwritten norms often rule the culture. Norms, which often were created by our shared experience and culture, have a way of blocking advancement for not only the individual but also the company. We must all continue to challenge ourselves and our colleagues to ensure policies, procedures, and behaviors are aligned with the growth mission of the organization.

Seldom is a mission for growth absent of diversity. There are entire books focused on the many dimensions of difference that make up our individual and group identities. We dedicated one chapter to highlighting the current dimensions of difference that figure most prominently in corporate discussion, and we spoke to their importance in an organizational context, the inherent challenges, and how to create inclusion for each aspect of difference.

Some of you may have wondered why this chapter is positioned relatively late in the book. Our philosophical approach to D&I is to focus on the foundational concepts of inclusion and behavior. These behaviors can then be applied universally regardless of the dimension of difference, which may change from culture to culture or even from department to department in a corporation. We understand that in the past the objective was to focus on key aspects of difference first and then on how to create inclusion. We have found that approach to be less effective in creating a systemic philosophy of inclusion for today's and tomorrow's differences. Although it is important to understand the inherent challenges in each dimension of difference, it is easier for leaders with leadership competencies in inclusion to incorporate these dimensions more effectively.

Up to this point, we provided insight and some helpful pointers to the realm of D&I. The last two chapters offer a straightforward prescriptive approach to taking these insights and forming leadership competencies as well as a sustainable D&I strategy. What is the good of awareness if you are not able to apply it to your reality? The word "sustainable" is paramount, as many initiatives, not just D&I, are not built to stand the test of time and eventual leadership change. There are a lot of tools in the D&I toolbox. Each tool has its own place and benefit in the strategy, and each has its own pitfalls if it is not utilized correctly. One approach may work in one environment but will not translate as evenly in another. Leaders need to achieve a level of competency and a strategy needs to be thoughtfully planned to fully realize a return.

Every chapter gave loads of numbers and examples on how investment in D&I provides a tangible return. However, these are someone else's numbers and examples. We urge you to view these examples as just that, examples. Leverage them for inspiration or guidance. You and your colleagues will need to discover your own inclusion dividend. To continue your learning journey, we suggest reading *SET for Inclusion: The Underlying Methodology for Achieving Your Inclusion Dividend*.

What is your inclusion dividend?

Email us at **Info@TheDagobaGroup.com.**

Index